Building Storage Stuff

Building Storage Stuff

25 Plans & Projects to Help Put Things in Their Place

Richard Freudenberger

Sterling Publishing Co., Inc.
New York
A STERLING/LARK BOOK

Art Director: Celia Naranjo
Photography: Evan Bracken and Spaarnestad Syndication—Holland
Production: Celia Naranjo
Illustrations: Don Osby
Production Assistant: Robert Gold

Library of Congress Cataloging-in-Publication Data
Freudenberger, Richard
    Building Storage Stuff : 25 projects to help put things in
their place/ Richard Freudenberger.
       p. cm.
    "A Sterling/Lark book."
    Includes index.
    ISBN 0-8069-9550-5
    1. Cabinetwork. 2. Shelving (Furniture) 3. Storage in the home.
I. Title.
TT197.F76   1997   97-379
684.1'6—dc21   CIP

10 9 8 7 6

A Sterling/Lark Book

Published by Sterling Publishing Co., Inc.
387 Park Ave. South
New York, NY 10016

Created and produced by Altamont Press, Inc.
50 College St.
Asheville, NC 28801

Photo opposite and those on pages 10–46 by Evan Bracken. All other photos
© Spaarnestad Syndication—Holland.

Special thanks to Craig Weis of *Architectural Woodcraft* for his time and expertise in
making possible the tool and wood shop photography.

Distributed in Canada by Sterling Publishing,
    c/o Canadian Manda Group
    One Atlantic Ave., Suite 105, Toronto, Ontario M6K 3E7, Canada
Distributed in Great Britain and Europe by Cassell PLC
    Wellington House, 125 Strand, London WC2R 0BB, England
Distributed in Australia by Capricorn Link (Australia) Pty. Ltd.
    P.O. Box 6651 Baulkham Hills Business Centre, NSW 2153,
    Australia

Printed in Hong Kong.
All rights reserved.

ISBN 0-8069-9550-5

table of contents

Introduction

Unlikely as it may seem for a title, "Storage Stuff" describes exactly what this book is all about. Who among us has not wished for more room to put the things that we've accumulated in even a short period of time? It's a trend! Doubters in any locale can take a quick walk through the Yellow Pages to confirm that mini-warehouses and personal storage units are not in any shortage.

Why this is may be beyond us, though you'll have to admit it's tough to ignore great-looking shopping catalogs or walk away from terrific yard sales.

How to handle it, however, is fully within our means. Houses built in a different time always seemed to have plenty of nooks and crannies to keep things in, secretive spaces to store things in, and quiet places to leave things in. These days, those things seem to find sustenance in stacks or spread across porches and flat surfaces.

No more. This book gets right to the root of the problem: Space isn't lacking, it's merely not being utilized well.

In these 144 pages, you'll discover how to make something of an empty spot, take advantage of a space you may never have noticed, or lay claim to those hazy zones where you weren't sure something would fit. Because the projects presented range from the very simple to the fairly involved, you don't have to start with anything overly ambitious—you can begin where you're comfortable and take it from there.

To make your planning a bit easier, the projects are grouped by the areas in which they'd most likely be used, although even a few moments spent in the pages should convince you that many of them could be used just about anywhere.

Some are quite straightforward, a place to hang your cups or file your flats and posters. Others are tucked into unlikely places—above the splashboard at the back of the kitchen counter or beneath the mattress slats of a unique bed. Still others are in truly found spaces—the built-in corner cabinet and window bench, the seasonal storage in the peak of the attic roof, and the utility trap beneath the stair landing.

There's no end to fresh ideas, and they're all here: a bookshelf built into a couch back, a bedfoot bin chest, a closet with self-contained dressers, hangers, shelves, and valets, and a wall unit bookcase that folds out to become a worktable. There are even a couple of mobile units that'll go anywhere your heart desires, and a garden workshop with all sorts of potential for outdoors.

And don't be discouraged if your woodworking experience leaves something to be desired. With even a small collection of hand and power tools, you'll be free—with the help of the seven instructional chapters that follow this introduction—to try your hand at any one of the clearly detailed and illustrated step-by-step projects presented in the book. If you have a shop already set up, you already have a head start and may even be comfortable making a few changes to what we've presented.

Chapter 1

planning and choosing a project

One of the most difficult things for a novice woodworker to get beyond is the barrier of design. For lack of a better way to put it, that's the fear of changing the plan even a little bit from what's been printed on paper.

Unfortunately, this reluctance can deny you a lot of pleasure if you allow it. For once you've mastered some basic woodworking techniques, there's no reason why you can't get creative. Perhaps you won't be ready to start your own project from scratch right away, but you should be able to make modifications from a plan without feeling like you're doing something wrong.

Nothing in this book, in fact, is carved in stone. You may wish to make a shelf longer or a cabinet taller to suit your situation. And, with the built-in projects especially, you will have to make changes just to accommodate the structure you have to work with.

Beyond that, even some of the techniques may be open to interpretation. You might want to use miter joints rather than butt joints in some instances, or you may wish to hang doors or mount shelves differently from what's shown. These, really, are minor deviations that we encourage.

Materials, too, are for the most part a matter of choice. We've specified a selection of sheet goods in the book because manufactured wood works well for the nature of these projects—many of them use pieces wider than a board's 11-1/4" practical limit. Yet, if you want to edge-join boards to make a wide solid-wood panel, or if you want to substitute cabinet-grade plywood for medium-density fiberboard, by all means have at it!

How you finish your projects will be determined to some degree by where you put them, and you shouldn't be hesitant to change your choice of building material to take advantage of a matching wood grain or color.

Where do you begin? If you feel more comfortable starting with something simple, use that as your criterion. Read over the cut lists and construction procedures to determine what you can handle and proceed with it.

If, on the other hand, you can see that a certain project would fit perfectly in your bedroom or attic, concentrate on that one. One of the yardsticks in putting this book together was to offer a variety of designs so that a homeowner, apartment dweller, or renter would be able to find something within the pages that he or she would be able to use.

One final word of advice: take some time to measure and contemplate your space before you charge ahead. Check for things such as projections into a walkway, door swings, height clearances, and practical matters of that nature prior to buying your first board.

And please—let caution prevail. With the built-in projects, keep in mind that there may be a live wire or water pipe behind that wall you're about to drill into. If you're not equipped to deal with the unknown, get some experienced help before you proceed with your work.

Chapter 2

your workshop and your safety

It matters very little whether you happen to be a beginning woodworker or an experienced hobbyist—organization is the key to woodworking success. How you arrange your tools, your work, and your raw materials will determine whether you'll enjoy yourself in the shop or will be constantly bogged down in retracing your footsteps, searching for misplaced tools, and moving things out of the way

As a beginner especially, when your work goes smoothly without a lot of frustrating interruptions, you feel comfortable about pursuing it. As you build up your confidence, your skills and projects tend to improve. Working with a core group of tools you feel easy around lets you start with the basics, and in due course become proficient with what you have.

A moderate tool selection can be fairly inexpensive and also takes up less room than a major collection. As you gain more experience, you can add tools to the lot as you find you need them, or as finances permit. You might want to budget in something new with each fresh project you tackle.

Try to avoid making major changes all at once. Something large like a stationary tool can really alter your shop's floor plan, and deserves some serious thought as to how it will be used effectively and efficiently without becoming a white elephant.

Taking Stock of Your Space

Those who already have a workshop of their own might want to just look through this chapter for fresh ideas—there's no telling what you might learn. If you don't have an area set up for woodworking, now's a good opportunity to plan a workable space.

Contrary to what you might think, size isn't necessarily the most important factor in setting up shop. The quality of your space—and how well you recognize and work with it—is the really important ingredient in bringing your workshop together.

The workshop area should be dry to protect not only your tools and hardware, but your working stock. Wood tends to swell in a damp environment, so any stock you store might be affected by moist conditions.

Ventilation is important if you don't have dust-collection equipment, or you plan on doing a lot of finishing work. A dust collector won't clear the air of harmful volatiles (the fumes that evaporate from a finish as it dries), but it will remove sawdust particles from around blades and sanders. A ventilating fan—even a window unit in a wall—will help to remove suspended dust and the fumes from drying finishes.

If your shop is terribly cold in the winter, you'll be tempted to stay out of it for most of the season, during which your tools will go unused. One solution is a portable space heater, but there can be some risk involved with that, too. Floating sawdust particles and fumes from finishing work can be dangerous in the presence of a heater's open flame. Here again, proper ventilation and dust collection will reduce the hazard.

Lighting should be from overhead and fluorescent if possible. Diffusers—the grates or covers you see over fluorescent tubes—can be a problem because they collect dust, but they also protect the glass tubes from breakage by flying wood chunks. Natural light from windows is fine if it's available, but most wood shops don't have that much glazing, and wall space taken up by a window just means less storage space.

Your site's electrical service should be adequate for the tools you have. If possible, tool outlets should be on a separate circuit from lighting, because even hand tools can draw a lot of amperage when they start. All breakers should be func-

Eye protection and a dust mask are two must-have items in the workshop.

tional, and the circuits grounded. A large stationary tool such as a table saw will have higher voltage and amperage needs and may need to be on its own circuit. If you blow fuses or kick breakers on a regular basis, the wiring is probably not heavy enough and needs to be upgraded. Don't simply replace the fuses or breakers with the next-higher amperage—that's how fires start.

Security in the home shop amounts to keeping doors and windows locked when you're not around, as much for curious children as for tool thieves. Covering windows with blinds or shutters is also a form of cheap insurance because it lessens temptation.

Arranging Your Tools

Any woodworking job calls for a basic selection of tools, some of which will be stationary if you've gotten serious about your hobby. Even a modest shop will most likely have a table saw, perhaps a radial-arm saw, and a workbench—which is as important a tool as anything else.

Your work will send you from tool to tool, and this motion should occur in a logical fashion. Woodworkers move between three areas: tool and material storage, stationary tool locations, and the workbench. These elements should be arranged in a pattern that will allow an open space in the center so you can move freely from place to place.

The shape of your workshop will determine the limits of these three points, creating a triangular work pattern. A square or rectangular shop is the most practical to work in. The workbench can be placed near the longest wall, and the standing tools against two adjacent walls. The remaining wall can be used for storage. Remember that both the table saw and workbench require some walking space around them to allow open access. A tool like the radial-arm saw or a band saw can be set up against a wall, with some working clearance at the sides.

A long and narrow space dictates a change from the triangular work pattern. In a situation such as this, a linear or in-line flow will function well as long as the workbench is centrally located so it becomes the focal point. Even if you put the bench against a wall, you'll still be able to access it from three sides. And if you place the items you use most frequently—measuring tools, hand-held power tools, and clamps—at the workbench and the middle of the shop, you'll save a lot of steps.

The Right Workbench

A sturdy bench provides a level surface where you can measure, clamp, glue, drill, and chisel—and it can provide some storage as well if there's a shelf underneath.

One feature of a good workbench is its stability; the heavier it is, the less likely it will be to shift as you work. You can reduce any movement by placing the bench against a solid wall, but at the cost of not being able to walk completely around it, which is a benefit worth considering.

Another detail that becomes important with larger projects is a level top. A warped surface will throw off the accuracy of corner joints and anything else that's meant to be square, because it's the only reference there is.

A good-quality workbench includes a vise, a well or relief for setting down tools, steel dogs (pegs set into holes in the top and used as stops for clamping), and solid stretchers between the legs for sturdy support. The top should be at or about 34", or close to hip height. Some benches come with adjustable leg hardware that allows a bit of up-and-down movement in addition to the normal leveling adjustment.

safety tips

Power tools can be dangerous if misused. Carelessness, haste, and ignorance are all the same to the saw—it will cut whatever gets in its way. And don't think that a tool must have teeth to be harmful. Just about any tool can cause injuries. The edge of a freshly sharpened chisel can quietly slice your finger, a shaper blade can launch a chunk of wood, and a sander can damage your respiratory system over time. Yet a carefully planned wood shop, treated with respect, can be as safe as your kitchen. The following guidelines will help you to establish that kind of shop.

✎ Keep your mind on your work, and pay attention to what's going on around you. Avoid distractions that can take you from the immediate task at hand.

✎ Unplug all power tools when making adjustments or changing blades and bits. This applies not only to hand-held tools such as routers and circular saws, but to the large stationary tools as well.

✎ Keep your workshop clean and tidy. Work surfaces cluttered with tools, extension cords lying loosely across the floor, and lumber supplies leaning here and there take time to maneuver around and invite trips and accidents

✎ Dress sensibly for woodworking. Loose cuffs and shirt sleeves, long hair left untied, and hanging jewelry are risky business around moving parts.

✎ Leave blade guards and other safety features in place. It's tempting (and sometimes necessary) to remove those parts to accommodate special jobs, but it's better to learn how to work with them.

✎ Always wear safety glasses or goggles. Glass or polycarbonate lenses must be impact-resistant; goggles are better than glasses because they provide protection at the sides of the eyes as well as at the front. Full-face shields are especially safe. Ear protection, too, is important in a noisy shop. Over-the-head muffs that reduce decibel levels by at least 25 dB are recommended, especially when working with noisy tools such as routers, saws, planers, and sanders.

✎ Dust protection cannot be ignored. Disposable dust masks are better than nothing at all, but a quality mask can be comfortable while filtering particles down to the recommended .5-micron level. For finishing work, where exposure to solvents and vapors are of particular concern, a working respirator, complete with .3-micron-level filter cartridges, is a reasonably-priced investment. Shop dust can be greatly reduced through the use of a dust collector connected by hose to each source, and kept under control by a window fan in the summer and a reasonably priced recirculating filtration system through the heating season.

✎ Avoid open flames in the wood shop. Cigarettes, pipes, and lighters are best left outside the work area. If you heat your shop with a space heater or room furnace (not through ductwork or radiators from elsewhere), keep in mind that flammable vapors from solvents, paints, and finishes are potentially combustible if left unvented. A 10-pound, A-B-C rated, dry-chemical fire extinguisher should be on hand at all times.

✎ Working on damp or wet floors can be an electrical, as well as a physical, hazard. All your tools should be double-insulated, and the ground circuit in your shop's wiring should be complete and functional.

Chapter 3

tools and more tools

This chapter is a defined list of the tools you'd probably use in woodworking—either to complete the projects in the book or to build projects and make renovations of your own design and style. Don't be put off by the number of tools listed—they're not all needed, though every one could be used if desired.

If you're a newcomer to woodworking, take your time and study the whole chapter closely, not only for safety's sake, but to understand what each tool is capable of doing. It's not difficult to make a considerable investment in tools, and while you certainly may not need every one on the list, you'll have to start with a basic collection of "old standards" to get the job done.

Those familiar with the working of wood will probably recognize that some of the tools listed are there to make the job go more quickly and with less effort. For a professional, a brisk pace might be the key to success, but a hobby woodworker should have the luxury of enjoying the work and the freedom to experiment with the wood and the tools alike. However, while hand tools are great to learn on, power tools take less out of you and are highly accurate besides.

Whether you're a novice or an expert, remember that you're the one who establishes a tool's real value. The best tools don't always make the best woodworker—if used poorly, even expensive items can be near useless. When buying new tools, invest in the best ones you can afford. But keep in mind that a woodworker with even a bit of experience under the belt can work miracles with modest tools.

Measuring and Marking Tools

Measuring and marking are essential to carpentry. No other part of the construction process has as much influence on the finished product as does the laying out of lengths, joints, and angles. Correctly marked and measured dimensions are critical, so don't deny the importance.

Measuring tools establish length, width, and depth. They're useful at the lumberyard to check stock dimensions, and they're absolutely necessary when you're building a woodworking project.

Marking tools are helpful in locating the lines, points, curves, and angles where you intend to cut, rout.

Steel Tape Measure

Steel tapes are long flexible rulers that roll up into a compact case. They're made in widths between 1/4" and 1" and in lengths from 6' to 25' or more. The tape end has a hook that secures to one end of the work; this should be loosely mounted to compensate for the width of the hook in both inside and outside measurements.

Graduations are noted in 1/16" increments (except for the first 12", which are marked in 1/32" increments). For most building projects, a 3/4"-wide, 16'-long, self-retracting rule with a tape-lock button is the best choice.

Straightedge

A straightedge—called a steel rule when marked with graduations—is very convenient for drawing straight lines. It's a steel or aluminum ruler, 12" to 36" long, which can be used for fine measuring and marking when graduated clearly.

Combination Square

The adjustable combination square is a 4-1/2" X 12" tool with a sliding blade, and a 45-degree shoulder built right into the stock. The blade can be locked at any point and its end used as a marking point for a scribe or sharp pencil.

Try Square

This small square is used to check, or "try," right angles; a ruler along the edge of its blade can be used to take quick measurements. The blades usually come in 6" to 12" lengths.

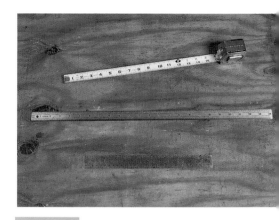

Accurate measurement is critical to good work. From top: steel tape, 24" straightedge rule, 12" steel rule.

A combination square with a built-in level and a graduated blade.

A pencil compass and a scratch awl are two elementary but important marking tools.

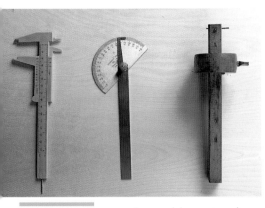

Some basic measuring tools. From left: vernier caliper, bevel protractor, and marking gauge.

The bench plane at top is used to remove wood from a broad surface; the block plane below is for spots and local work.

Even a small thickness planer can pay for itself many times over if you work with a lot of rough-sawn mill stock.

Framing Square

A framing square is shaped like a large right angle and is used to check for 90-degree accuracy on a large scale. Its two edges are 16" x 24" long and are marked with ruler graduations in 1/8" and 1/16" increments. The framing square is used mainly in construction carpentry.

Scratch Awl

A scratch awl is a hard steel point several inches in length, with a comfortable rounded handle. Its intended use is to mark a starting point for a drill bit, but sharpened awls are often used to score a line for marking or cutting. Another tool, the scribe, is a finer version of the instrument in a slightly different form.

Marking Gauge

A marking gauge is used to scribe a line at a point in relation to an edge. Its hardwood stock holds a graduated inch-scale beam which slides through its center. The beam is locked in position with a thumbscrew, and a steel spur at the end marks the wood when the gauge is pushed along the work.

Compass

A compass has a pivot at the top and two legs, one with a pointed end and one with a pencil tip. This tool is used to scribe and transfer radius

arcs, circles, and patterns during the layout process.

Protractor

A woodworker's protractor is a simple tool used to determine angles. It has a head with a flat base, upon which a pivoting blade is attached. The blade is aligned with the angle, which is then indicated in degrees on a graduated scale etched into the head.

Vernier Caliper

The vernier caliper is a refined thickness gauge used to measure the thickness of a piece of wood up to 5", in sixteenths of an inch and in millimeters. A slide bar gives a linear readout and also may include an end rod for depth measurement. An extra set of calipers allows for measuring inside dimensions.

Level

A level is used to establish whether a framing member is level (if it's horizontal), or plumb (if it's vertical). It uses a bubble captured within a small tube of liquid to determine the degree off of "center" the object in question may be. A long, thin frame of aluminum or wood houses three bubble vials, two at the end positioned to read for plumb, and one in the center set to read for level. For accurate work, a level at least 24" in length is needed.

Plumb Bob

This tool is simply an 8-ounce weight with a sharp point connected to a nylon line. When suspended from an overhead point, it's used to transfer that point's position to the ground or a framing member below.

Planing Tools

Planes are used to bring down the thickness or width of wood stock to a uniform level. In special projects, some of the better wood—especially if it's not a common commercial species—might be rough-cut or surfaced (planed) on one or two sides only. It's up to you to custom-size your own stock unless you have a wood shop to do it for you.

Bench Plane

A hand-held tool with a blade set at an angle within a steel frame. The edge of the blade is adjusted to protrude slightly from a slot in the sole, or base, of the body. The variety of hand planes, and the jobs they do, is enormous—but for general shop work, a plane with a 1-3/4" to 2" blade and a sole 9" to 10" long is ideal.

Other planes may be mentioned in the instructions for the individual projects. A block plane is a small, hand-sized plane with a 2" X 6" body used for detail work.

Power Plane

This is a hand-held power tool made to plane large amounts of stock from a board's surface quickly. A typical power plane has a two-edged rotary blade about 3-1/4" wide and a sole between 10" and 12" long. Depending on its horsepower and the speed of its rotary cutter, a power plane can remove from 1/32" to 1/16" of wood in each pass.

Thickness Planer

A stationary tool used to plane rough-cut boards to a uniform thickness. A portable or "benchtop" planer is relatively inexpensive and can handle boards up to 12" wide and 6" thick, removing a maximum of 1/16" of material with each pass.

A larger standing stationary planer can be three to six times more costly, and accommodate a board up to 20" wide and 8" thick. Higher-amperage or 220-volt service might be needed for these larger tools.

Jointer

A large standing tool designed to level the face of a board and put a consistent and accurate edge on it in preparation for making a joint. A saw blade by itself cannot make a perfectly accurate cut because there's no true reference on a warped board to work from.

Benchtop jointers exist, but most jointers are stand-mounted and built to handle boards 6" to 8"

A jointer can surface both face and edge of a board. It can also cut a rabbet if set up correctly.

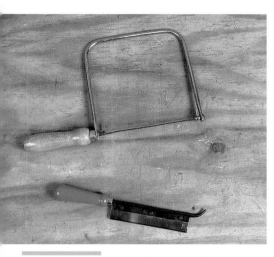

A *coping saw and the thumbsaw, a small version of a backsaw.*

A *compact miter box and a small backsaw is all that's needed for most trim work.*

wide. A large fence designed to tilt right and left, 45 degrees each direction, allows the cutting of beveled edges. The better jointers have a 1/2" depth of cut and the ability to complete a 1/2" rabbet.

Cutting Tools

The function of a saw is determined by the number, pitch, bevel, and angle of teeth on its blade. The higher the number of teeth per inch of blade (a measurement given in "points"), the smoother the blade's cut will be. A saw with fewer points will make a coarser cut, but it will also cut more quickly. A backsaw, for instance, with 15 teeth per inch, is used for fine joinery work; a crosscut saw, given 8 teeth per inch, can make rapid cuts across thick lumber.

Power saws often use what are known as combination blades, which offer clean cuts both with and against the wood's grain. Various other blades are made to cut sheet metal, composites, plywood, fiberboard, and other sheet products.

Crosscut Saw

A crosscut saw is used to cut across or against the wood's grain. Though crosscut saw lengths vary, a 26" version will work well for any hand-sawing you do, except through plywood. Crosscut saws are available with 7 through 12 points per inch, depending on how coarse or fine you

wish the cut to be. The greater the number, the smoother the cut, and the more slowly it will be made.

Ripsaw

A ripsaw is designed to cut with or along the wood's grain. Most ripsaws are 26" long and come with 4-1/2 through 7 points per inch. If you work without power saws, you'll want to own both a ripcut and a crosscut saw. While it is possible to rip with a crosscut saw, you can't make a cross cut with a ripsaw.

Backsaw

A fine-toothed handsaw used in joinery to make smooth, accurate cuts. The steel back frame fastened to the uppermost edge of the blade stiffens it and gives the saw its name. Backsaws can range in size from 4" to about 14" in length, and go under different names such as thumb, gentleman's, and tenon saw, depending on their purpose.

Coping Saw

The steel-bow frame of a coping saw is "U" shaped. A very thin blade, with 10 to 12 teeth per inch, is mounted between the tips of the U. This saw is especially useful for cutting curves because its frame can be angled away from the line of cut. It is designed to cut boards generally thinner than 3/4".

Miter Box

A wooden or metal frame used in conjunction with a backsaw to hand-cut miters in boards and trim. Specially designed compound miter boxes allow beveled miter cuts as well.

Circular Saw

The motor-driven, hand-held circular saw has a 7-1/4" blade which can be adjusted to cut at angles between 90 degrees and 45 degrees. When set to cut at a perpendicular, blade penetration is 2-1/4"; at 45 degrees, it's reduced to 1-3/4". The greatest drawback to a circular saw is that it's heavy and unwieldy, which affects its accuracy.

Better-quality circular saws are usually equipped with a carbide-tipped combination blade, but regular blades will do just as well if you sharpen or replace them regularly. A good blade can be installed on an inexpensive saw to improve its performance.

Compound Miter Saw

Sometimes called a chop saw or cutoff saw, this is a portable power tool that's evolved through several stages. The least expensive version is similar to a circular saw, but mounted on a short table with a pivoting hinge. It pulls down to cut, and can be swung right and left 45 degrees to cut miters. The next level includes a beveling feature that lets the blade

tilt as well, allowing a compound bevel cut. The best model uses a slide mount so the blade and motor can be pulled down and forward up to 12", much like a radial-arm saw, and can cut miters and bevels as well. Blade diameters range from 8-1/2" to 12".

Radial-Arm Saw

A stationary tool used to cross-cut long pieces of stock on a large fixed table. It uses a powerful motor and 10" blade suspended on a carriage from a beam which can be swung right and left, and raised and lowered as well. The blade can also be tilted to make bevel cuts. A pivot in the carriage allows the motor and blade to be turned 90 degrees for making rip cuts as well.

Table Saw and Dado Blade

The table saw uses a heavy motor built into a frame and table. It's weight and design gives a more accurate cut than a hand-held circular saw can deliver. The typical table saw has a pivoting carriage that holds the blade's arbor, or axle. This construction allows the blade to be raised to a 90-degree cutting depth of 3-1/8"—and tilted up to 45 degrees, which gives a 2-1/8" cut at that angle.

Generally, table saws are equipped with a 10" carbide-tipped combination blade. Compact and portable table saws that use smaller

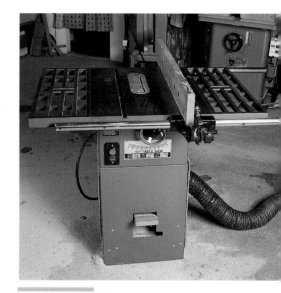

The table saw is the basic workhorse of the wood shop.

A *chipper-style dado blade* installed in the table saw.

A jigsaw can cut straight and beveled edges in a straight line or a radiused curve.

Even a sizeable collection of clamps doesn't represent a big investment. From left: spring clamps, C-clamp, bar clamps, pipe clamps, handscrew.

blades, but which have the same features as the larger models, are also manufactured.

Table saws come with a rip fence, a long, straight bar that runs parallel to the exposed blade and can be adjusted to either side of it. The fence assures accurate rip cuts by guiding material into the blade.

A miter gauge, which is adjustable to 45 degrees on either side of its 90-degree midpoint, helps in making miter cuts by holding the stock at the correct angle as it's passed through the blade.

A dado blade is a specially designed cutting tool that's fitted to a table saw to make wide grooves and notches. There are two common dado designs. One uses an offset blade that wobbles to the right and to the left as it revolves. The other type uses two outer blades and a number of inner "chippers" that are stacked side by side to establish the exact width of the cut.

Jigsaw

The hand-held jigsaw, sometimes called the saber saw, is the powered alternative to a coping saw and is used to cut curves, free-form shapes, and large holes in panels or boards up to 1-1/2" thick. Cutting action is provided by a narrow, reciprocating bayonet-style blade which moves very rapidly. A shoe surrounding the blade can be tilted 45 degrees to the right and left of perpendicular for angled cuts.

The best jigsaws have a variable speed control and an orbital blade action; this action swings the cutting edge forward into the work and back again, through the blade's up-and-down cycle. A dust blower keeps the cut clear, and the tool may also come with a circle cutting guide and rip fence as well.

Utility Knife

This inexpensive tool can be used to cut thin wood and material, and to scribe lines for marking. The best kinds have two or three blade positions, including fully retractable for safety.

Clamping Tools

Clamps are used to hold parts to each other or to a bench so that you can mark, drill, or cut them, and they also serve to hold glued parts together as the glue dries. Used with strips of wood, clamps can be made into saw and router guides or extended to clamp over a large area.

C-Clamps

C-clamps get their name from the basic "C" shape of their steel frames. One end of the "C" (the anvil) is fixed; it doesn't move at all. The other end is fitted with a threaded rod and swivel pad. When the threaded end is tightened, whatever is between it and the fixed end is tightly gripped. Pads or scraps of wood should be used between the jaws and your work so that the work isn't marred when the clamp is tightened.

C-clamps come in a variety of styles and sizes, but in general they're small; woodworking C-clamps are usually limited to a 12" jaw opening, but for the projects in this book, a 4" or 6" size is fine.

Bar and Pipe Clamps

These clamps are made to span long or wide pieces of wood frame, panels, or doors, or to grip several pieces of wood that are placed edge-to-edge. Their frames are simply steel or aluminum bars, or sections of iron plumbing pipe that are several feet in length. At one end is a fixed head, equipped with a short, threaded rod and a metal pad. At the other end is a sliding tail stop which can be locked in any position along the bar or pipe to accommodate the work.

Pipe clamps are less expensive, but more flexible, than bar clamps, and can be made 6' or more in length. Pipe-clamp kits are sold that include only the fixtures; you purchase the pipe and have its end threaded at a local plumbing supply store.

Vises

A vise is just a bench-mounted clamp. It can be used to hold work pieces together or to hold stock securely while you work on it. A woodworker's vise has smooth,

broad jaws which are usually drilled so that facings can be installed to prevent marring fine work. Better wood vises include a dog; this is a bar that slides up from the vise's movable jaw to hold work against a similar stop mounted on the bench itself. The dog extends the vise's effective jaw opening by 24" or more. Some vises also make use of a half-nut to provide quick-slide opening and closing; tightening occurs only once the work is in place.

Drilling and Boring Tools

Cutting clean holes through wood requires the use of drills and bits suited for the job. Holes can be functional or designed with special features such as a tapered counter-sink opening or an internal shoulder.

3/8" Variable–Speed Reversible Drill

Though you can bore almost any hole with a hand drill, there's little reason not to own this versatile power tool, which operates more quickly and with less effort than a manually operated drill. For most any project, a drill with a 3/8" chuck capacity and a motor amperage of 3.5 amps or greater will do just fine. Cordless versions are made and are good for driving screws and drilling small holes, but they may not be suitable for continuous, heavy-duty work.

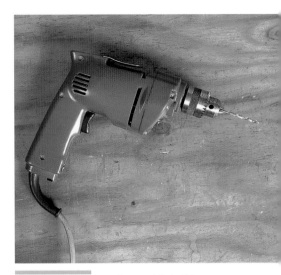

The 3/8" variable-speed reversible drill has more power than a cordless model, but isn't as convenient because of the cord.

A 3/8" cordless reversible drill is perfect for general drilling and screw-driving jobs.

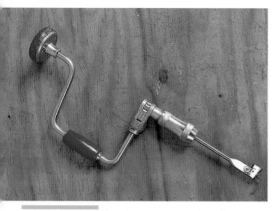

A hand brace fitted with an expansion bit. This is a versatile tool that's often overlooked by woodworkers comfortable with power equipment.

Forstner bits are designed to cut clean, perfect holes or counterbores.

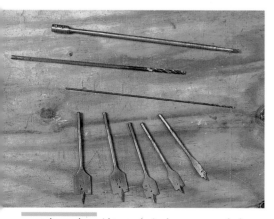

Specialty tools and bits include the extension shaft and two extension bits above, and a set of spade bits below.

At a small extra cost, you can get an electric drill with a variable-speed control. This feature allows you to govern the speed of the drill's motor by simply varying the pressure you exert on the tool's trigger. A reversible motor is included with this option, which permits you to take screws out just as quickly as you insert them.

Stop Collars

When you need to control the depth of a drill bit's penetration, use a stop collar. These are metal (or sometimes plastic) rings that tighten onto the drill bit's shaft. When the bit sinks into the wood, the collar hits the wood's face and stops the bit from going any deeper. Stop collars are sized to fit different drill-bit diameters.

Countersinks

A project's appearance and function can suffer when the head of a screw protrudes above the face of the wood. In order to hide these heads, a countersink is used. These angle-faced bits cut shallow, slope-sided holes into the surface of the work, creating a recess into which the screw's head rests, flush with the face of the work.

Brace and Bit

This is a two-handed drill that operates like a crank. At the top end is a handle that allows the crank to pivot and keeps it in line. At the lower end, a two-jawed chuck grips a spiral boring bit, or some type of expansion bit. The working hand turns the grip on the crank to slowly bore the opening. A brace is especially useful for drilling deep or large-diameter holes cleanly and accurately.

Specialty Bits

A variety of drill bits are made to accomplish specific tasks. Forstner bits are used to drill clean, flat-bottomed holes when a fine cut is called for. They are made in 1/4" to 2-1/4" diameters. Spade bits (used with power drills) bore quickly and make rough but effective holes through wood. They're designed with a center point and two flat cutting edges and come in 1/4" to 1-1/2" diameters.

Screw bits are countersink/pilot drills that combine the hole-drilling and countersinking processes in one operation. The better versions of these bits use what's known as a tapered bit, which follows the contour of a standard wood screw; they also include a stop collar. These combination bits are made for screw size Nos. 5 through 12. This type of drill bit is partcularly versatile because it allows the woodworker to countersink a fastener flush with the wood's surface, or to counterbore the hole to give the screw a deeper penetration where desirable.

Extension bits, and extension shafts made to fit spade and other types of power bits, allow you to bore holes deeper than a normal-length bit would allow. The extra-length bits come in diameters from 3/16" to 3/4" and usually are 18" long; the spade bit extension shafts come in 18" and 24" lengths and are made to fit standard 5/16" and 7/16" power-bit shanks.

Chiseling and Routing Tools

Joinery and decorative work both rely on tools that are able to make sharp, detailed cuts, or create consistent shapes along an edge or on the face of a piece of wood. Regardless of whether these tools are hand- or machine-operated, they use a sharp cutting edge to do their work.

Chisels

The standard mortise chisel is fine for most general woodworking projects. This cabinetmaker's tool is used to clean up joints and mortises, shave glue and grain from a joint, or simply remove layers of wood from one spot. A set of four or five bevel-edge chisels for hand or mallet work, in sizes from 1/4" to 1" wide, is a good choice.

Routers

A router's job is to cut grooves and rabbets, shape edges, and make slots, and it does that work easily and quickly. Rounded or chamfered edges can be cut with a router and a roundover or chamfer bit. Similar edges can be cut with gouges, rasps, and sanders, but it takes some time and often results in visible incosistencies.

Router bits are held in a collet on the end of a shaft, which in turn is supported by a flat base and housing. The shape of the bit determines what type of cut will be made in the work, and handles on the housing allow the operator to control the direction of the bit.

The simplest routers have 3/8" collets, external clamp-depth controls, and low-amperage motors. More sophisticated models are known as plunge routers; these allow vertical entry into the work for precise cutting and have 1/2" collets, variable-speed 12- to 15-amp motors, and variable-depth controls.

In a better-equipped workshop, routing work is done on a router table, which is just a stand with a cast surface that uses a heavy-duty 1/2" router inverted and mounted from the bottom. An adjustable fence and a special see-through guard allow you to guide the work through the exposed bit safely.

A shaper is a stationary routing tool that uses a powerful motor and a 1/2" or 3/4" spindle to handle work beyond the capability of a table-mounted router—such as moldings, heavy raised panels, and hardwood trim.

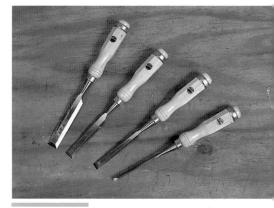
A small set of cabinet chisels for mortise and clean-up work.

A 1/2" plunge router fitted with a cove bit. The motor and collet can be lowered into the work.

The shape of the cutting edges on these 1/2" router bits determines the profile of the wood once it's cut. The small bearings help guide the bits.

The biscuit joiner cuts slots in adjoining members which are filled with a single strong wafer.

A hardwood bench mallet and a small claw hammer, for driving brads.

Router Bits

The design and shape of a router bit dictates what form the finished edge or groove will take. There are over 200 router-bit styles available for various types of work, though for the projects in this book only a few may be needed. When cutting or shaping an edge, a router bit with a ball-bearing pilot at its tip is used. The tip rolls along the edge below the part of the wood being cut, assuring a high degree of accuracy.

Groove- or slot-cutting bits cannot use pilot tips, so a guide or temporary fence is often used when routing a channel. This guide is a device that clamps onto the base of the tool and acts as a moving fence to keep the router and bit following the edge of the work.

Either type of bit is set vertically by adjusting the router base to control the depth of cut.

Laminate Trimmers

The high-pressure laminates used to cover countertops and other surfaces need special cutting equipment that doesn't shatter or chip the material's delicate edges. Though you probably won't be using laminate products unless you've had some experience with them, it's nice to know how they're managed.

Motorized laminate trimmers are basically compact routers with special bits and bases designed to cut perfect seams and edge joints in surface laminates and veeners.

A hand-held trimmer is a small block with one or two blades that fits around the edge of a board to cut the banding that covers the edge so it meets the surfaces without gaps or high spots.

Joining Tools

Once boards and components are prepared for joining, several tools can be used to complete the joint. Small backsaws and chisels are the traditional means of doing this, but newer methods have also developed in the interest of saving time.

Doweling Jig

This is a precision frame used to center holes on the edge of a board up to about 2" thick. Various-sized holes correspond to the diameter of the dowels being used, and the jig allows these holes to be placed exactly on the mating pieces, so the edges of the joined boards are aligned both vertically and horizontally. It's used mainly for edge-joining and certain framing applications.

Biscuit Joiners

The biscuit, or plate, joiner is just a high-speed rotary saw with a blade about 4-1/8" in diameter and 4mm thick. The cutter is set on a vertical axis so it cuts horizontally as it plunges into the edge of the work. An adjustable miter fence permits joinery on square and beveled edges, and a depth adjuster sets the plunge level to correspond with the size of biscuit to be used. There are three different sizes of biscuits (Nos. 0, 10, and 20) which range in length from 2-1/8" to 2-9/16" and in width from 1-1/8" to 1-7/8".

Hammering and Setting Tools

Hammers

The hammer you'll probably use in finishing work is a lightweight tack hammer, 3-1/2 or 6 ounces in weight. A claw style will do, but even better is a Warrington hammer because it has one traditional flat face and one elongated peen for starting the small brads used to set trim.

Nail set

A nail set is simply a fine-pointed punch used to set the head of a finishing nail or brad below the surface of the wood without enlarging the nail hole.

Mallets

If you need a larger hammer for chisel work or setting joints, an 8" wooden carpenter's mallet of 12 ounces or so would do well. Plastic-

headed mallets are also used for this type of work.

Screwdriving Tools

The screw fasteners used throughout the book have a No. 2 Phillips head, which gives a positive and usually slipless grip. Larger Phillips-head screws (No. 12 and up) are driven with a No. 3 Phillips screwdriver tip.

Screwdrivers

A screwdriver can come with a variety of tips, but a 6" or 8" No. 2 Phillips driver with a molded or wooden handle is the one to use on the No. 6, No. 8, and No. 10 Phillips-head screws usually used in this book's projects.

If you choose to use traditional slotted screws, a 3/16" and a 1/4" straight blade are needed. Square-drive screw heads naturally use square-tip drivers.

Power Drivers

Most woodworkers use power-drive bits in combination with cabinet or drywall screws to save time. These bits—used with hand-held drivers or 3/8" variable-speed power drills—have a short, six-sided shank which slips easily into the drill chuck. The tip can be a Phillips or straight-bladed design, though a square-drive tip to fit matching screws is another option.

Power driver bits. From left: square drive, No. 2 Phillips, 5/16" and 3/8" hex head.

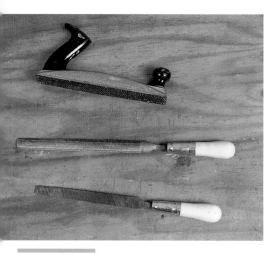

Rasps and files are used to bring down high spots and contour edges and corners.

Abrasives are used to smooth wood for finishing. The sanding block and pad at left are hand tools; the block is fitted with paper such as the aluminum oxide sheet at right.

Sanding and Smoothing Tools

To properly finish a piece of wood, it's often necessary to level surfaces by removing material, and to smooth the grain. Files and rasps cut or round edges and small areas; sandpaper prepares the wood for its final finish.

Rasps and Files

Wood rasps are coarse-cutting hand tools used to make the first cut in removing wood stock for shaping or rounding. A finer cabinet rasp is made for second-cut work. Rasps come in three styles: flat on both sides, half-round on one side, and round.

Wood files are less coarse than rasps and are used for finer smoothing and finishing work. Like rasps, they're about 10" long; they usually come in round and half-round cross sections.

For the projects in this book, only a flat rasp might be needed. But in general, two grades of files are good to have on hand. These are a 10" or 12" bastard-cut file, one step finer than a coarse file, and with a half-round back which allows it to be used on inside curves and arcs; For finish work, a smooth-cut file, which is the least coarse of the group, and especially suited to hardwoods.

Sanders and Sandpaper

Sanding can be done by hand or with power sanders. If you choose to sand by hand, you'll want to purchase a hand-sanding block.

The hand-held orbital finishing sander—called a palm or pad sander—has a palm grip and either a round or square pad to which sandpaper is attached. The orbiting mechanism uses a 2-amp motor to be effective. For convenience, the round styles use self-adhesive paper on the pad rather than mechanical clips.

Sandpaper and the replaceable pads for palm sanders come in a variety of grits to indicate the size of the abrasive particles on the paper: coarse (No. 60), medium (No. 80), fine (No. 150), and very fine (No. 220). Other finer grits are also manufactured. Standard garnet paper is suitable for woodwork and is unique in that the abrasive particles continuously break away, exposing fresh material as they do; aluminum-oxide sanding sheets, however, are more durable and less likely to clog up with waste.

Dust Collectors

Sawdust can be an irritant and even a hazard over time. A dust mask or respirator will filter material, but a shop dust collector will remove sawdust at the source and contain it in a canister for later disposal. A moderate investment will allow you to move air at 500 or 600 cubic feet per minute through a 4" tube from a single source.

Chapter 4

easy woodworking techniques

If you're new to woodworking, this chapter is for you. The previous chapter dealt with the tools you'd most likely be using in working with the projects. The next few pages contain a simple and basic description of the tool-working techniques used and described throughout the book, and also include some definitions of common woodworking terms.

If your woodworking skills are very basic, you can get comfortable with the terminology and pick up new techniques by reading over this section carefully. Woodworkers with more experience can review it, too, to brush up on techniques that are sometimes taken for granted.

Careful measurement gets the work off to the right start. Even 1/16" can be critical.

Measuring and Marking

Careful layout and measurement are as fundamental to good woodworking as is using the correct tools. You shouldn't use a tape measure to mark a straight line, or rely on a square blade to make a circle. Likewise, it's important to stick with the same tools through the completion of the project—switching tapes or marking gauges in midstream is the cause of many small mistakes.

Usually, the steel tape is the basis of all measuring activity. Most general measuring jobs go to the tape because it's fast and accurate within 1/16"—acceptable for almost any but the finest of woodworking projects.

But a steel tape can't strike a straight line over any distance. The metal band will move or distort no matter how careful you are. For distances less than 36", a straightedge is the best choice if you need to mark a line.

As an option, you can always use a chalk line—a chalked string stretched between two points—or you can use the tape to mark short increments over a greater distance, then strike lines between them with a straightedge if need be.

When marking for a cut, traditional woodworkers often use only a steel scribe or a pointed awl tip. But a sharp pencil can still make a very accurate V-shaped mark, which works well because the point of the V shows right where to cut.

Marking a square or perpendicular edge is the job of a square. This is necessary for marking crosscuts or transferring a line to the remaining three sides of a board. A try square does the job best on smaller pieces, a framing square on the larger ones. Use it by laying the stock, or handle, of the tool against the edge of the work, and marking, in pencil, a line along the blade. To transfer the line to the side and back surfaces, walk the square around the work, using the tail of the previous line as the start of the next one, and so on.

To lay out a radius of partial or full circles, use a compass. Open its legs to the correct radius, then place the point at the center of the circle or arc you wish to make and swing the other leg to make the mark. Remember that the radius is half a circle's width, while the diameter is its full width.

Figuring angles can be difficult, but the job is simplified with a protractor. The standard transparent type or the stainless steel kind with degree-graduations along the edge are both fine. Lay the bottom along the work's baseline and the measurement can be read at the top arc. But the more sophisticated bevel protractor has a pivoting arm that can be laid alongside the angle as well, making it easier to read or establish the existing angle or bevel.

A level is used to establish the degree off of "plumb" (straight up-

and-down) or "level" (horizontally straight) of a framing member. The level's frame is laid against the side or top of the member, and the position of the bubble within the appropriate vial tells you how true the piece is. A centered bubble indicates perfect accuracy. For plumb measurement, the end vials are used; for determining level, the center one is read.

Cutting Straights and Curves

After you've done the measuring and marking, making the cuts is a matter of following the lines. Double-check your measuring work, because once a cut is made, it cannot be corrected.

When using a handsaw, grip it firmly—but not tensely—with the back of the handle squarely against the ball of your palm. Guide the teeth with the outer edge of your thumb when starting a cut, which should be made on the waste, or outer, side of the line. A cut is always started on the upstroke, and the sides of the blade must be kept square with the surface of the wood.

With crosscuts, the tool should be held at a 45-degree angle; with rip cuts, the process works better at 60 degrees. The cutting pressure should be delivered only on the downstroke.

When using a circular saw, make sure the blade depth is set—by loosening a knob and moving the shoe up or down—so the teeth fully penetrate the opposite face of the work. This clears sawdust particles and makes the blade less likely to jam. Also, make sure your sawhorse or workbench is out of the way of the blade, or you'll cut it along with your work.

Set up in a comfortable position before starting the saw, but not so far forward that you'll be off balance at the end of a long cut. Don't grip the handle too tightly, because it'll make your hand tired and may throw off the accuracy of your work. The larger saws come with a second grip at the front for added control, but remember that two-handed sawing requires that you clamp your work down before cutting.

Always wear safety glasses when using any saw. Draw the power cord behind you before starting the tool, and sight your line of cut along the reference mark on the front of the saw's shoe. The safety guard will swing up by itself as you move the tool forward.

A table saw can cut more precisely than a circular type because it has a guide fence and a miter gauge. The cutting depth is set with the handwheel located at the front of the saw cabinet; the blade should penetrate the work enough that several full teeth are exposed during the cut, as this cools the blade and allows the sawdust to escape.

To adjust the fence, loosen the lock and slide the fence to the right

Often a straightedge or guide board is used to ensure a straight panel cut.

or left as needed. You can use the gauge on the fence rails for measuring the width of cut, but a more accurate method is to take a steel-tape reading between the fence's edge and the tip of a blade tooth that's set toward the fence.

After starting the motor, allow it a few seconds to come up to speed; never shove a piece of wood into a slowly moving blade. Don't ever put your hands near the spinning blade; use a push stick about 18" in length to pass the work through.

A thin–bladed coping saw is the basic curve–cutting tool for thinner material and very tight contours because it's easily controlled. If the stock is more than 3/8" or so in thickness, or the line greater than the throat depth of the saw, a hand–held electric jigsaw is a better choice. The tighter the curve or circle, the thinner the jigsaw blade should be so it doesn't bind or overheat.

Cutting at an angle, as when making miters and bevels, can be done in several ways. A miter is an angle–cut made across the face of a board, as in the corners of a picture frame. A bevel is an angle cut into the edge of a board, as in a piece of trim or molding. And a compound cut is a combination of both. If the wood is less than 6" or so in width, a miter box used with a fine backsaw gives the most accurate miter cut.

The shoe on a circular saw can be adjusted to a 45–degree angle for bevel cutting. For greater accuracy, the table saw blade can be adjusted to the same degree by using the handwheel on the side of the cabinet.

To make a miter cut on the table saw, loosen the knob on the miter gauge and adjust its fence to the desired angle, then tighten the knob. By holding the work against the fence, both the gauge and the work can be moved forward to meet the blade.

Rabbets and grooves can be cut with a table saw fitted with a dado blade, though with many projects it's easier to make them using a router and a straight bit. To use the saw for this procedure, remove the table insert and set the dado head width.

This can be done in one of two ways, depending on the blade design. The offset "wobbler" type has a rotating hub that changes the width by altering the blade's degree of offset. The stacked type must be set up out of the saw and reinstalled on the arbor. When you stack the chippers between the outer blades, make sure that the teeth rest between the gullets of the adjacent blades and that the chippers are staggered around the circumference.

Adjust the depth of the blade with the handwheel and set the fence to establish the position of the rabbet or groove on the work. Don't try to cut too quickly because the blade must work hard as it is to remove so much wood at one time.

On thick pieces of stock, a jigsaw makes cutting along curved lines an easy task. A thin blade can follow a fairly tight radius.

Grooving and Joining

Mortises and mortised hinges require that you clean and straighten surfaces that haven't been fully cut with a saw or drill. This is the chisel's job, and it will go easily as long as the tool has a consistently sharp edge.

On most work, you won't need to use a mallet; hold the chisel in your right hand to provide the push, and guide the blade with the left to control direction. If you do use a mallet, strike the tool lightly so as to avoid taking big bites at once. Work with the grain and hold the tool at a slight right or left angle whenever possible, because this makes the smoothest cut and is less likely to dull the blade. To avoid gouging the work, don't drive the edge too steeply—hold the blade at a slight downward angle.

For deeper cuts or shaping work, a router can handle quickly and cleanly what would take some time with a saw and chisel. The shape of the router bit's cutting surfaces determine what the finished edge or groove will look like. A straight bit makes a slot the width of the bit itself; a roundover bit cuts a clean, rounded edge into a squared surface; a chamfer bit cuts a beveled edge; and a ogee cuts a detailed profile.

When operating a router, you should grasp it comfortably in both hands and position yourself to get a clear look at the working bit—be sure to wear eye protection. The rule is to move it from left to right; if circular or irregular cutting is needed, then the motion should be counterclockwise. It's best to make any cuts across the end grain of your work first, then with the grain to avoid chipping.

The base of the router is loosened and the motor housing adjusted up or down to control the depth of cut. Before making any permanent cuts, you should run a test on a piece of scrap wood to see what your work will look like. Practice will improve your control of the tool, and after a while, you'll begin to rely on the depth gauge marked on the side of the router rather than having to test every cut you make.

Freehand work is fine for short jobs, or when the bit has an attached pilot bearing, but when making long cuts, you'll probably need to clamp the wood to a bench and use the tool's base–mounted guide to keep the cut straight. If you don't have a guide, you can usually substitute by clamping a straight section of 1 X 2 to the bench or your work, parallel to the line you wish to cut.

To rout narrow stock or edge–rabbet grooves, you'll need to place a piece of scrap stock to the right and left of the work, flush with the working surface. This will prevent the router base from tilting to one side and spoiling the cut, and will give you a place to mount a guide if you use one.

A 1/2" *plunge router edge-rounding a piece of medium-density fiberboard.*

Drilling and countersinking is a one-step process, when using a screw bit.

Drilling and Countersinking

There are three parts to a screw hole: the pilot or lead hole (which is a little more than half the diameter of the screw itself), the shank or body hole (the same diameter as the screw), and the sink or bore, used if the screw head is to be recessed below the surface of the wood.

In softwoods, it's not really necessary to drill more than just the pilot hole for a short screw. Dense hardwoods and long screws sometimes call for a shank hole, too. Make that hole only as deep as the shank—the unthreaded portion of the screw—is long. Also, remember that screws driven into wood's end–grain have less than half the holding power of a screw driven perpendicular to the grain.

Combination countersink and pilot bits, called screw bits, simplify hole–drilling considerably. They're sized by screw numbers, and their stop collars and countersinks are adjustable for length. They use specially tapered bits that accommodate standard wood screws perfectly.

Cabinet screws are even easier to use in some situations, as when driving into softwoods using 1–1/2" or shorter No. 6 and No. 8 diameters. These are self–tapping power–driven screws that don't need pilot holes, though you should take care to predrill the pilots when working near the end of the wood.

Another variation known as deck screws are coated with a smooth anodization which makes them weather–resistant. They'll work in softwoods and hardwoods, but the screw holes should be predrilled for harder wood or you may split the wood or shear the screw head off.

Drilling socket holes can be done with a regular drill bit if the diameters are small enough—1/4" or 3/8". A hole larger than that needs a Forstner bit, which produces a clean, flat–bottomed hole. A stop collar or a piece of tape can be used on a standard drill bit if you feel you may have trouble gauging the depth of a socket correctly.

Drilling through–holes takes some care in not tearing out the back side of the work, especially if another piece is planned to face it. You can avoid splintering wood this way by drilling only partially through the piece, then coming at the hole from the opposite side. Using a small pilot bit to penetrate the back face helps to locate the point at which to start the second hole.

Clamping

Most of the clamps used in woodworking function to hold parts together while they're being glued. They can also secure pieces for cutting or drilling.

Bar or pipe clamps are especially suited for wide clamping jobs because they're long and relatively inexpensive for their size. A sliding tailpiece permits a large range of adjustment between the jaws.

In the case of joints or pieces less than 12" in depth, a C–clamp is the logical choice. These clamps come in standard and deep throat depths, but they all have a threaded rod with a swivel tip that applies pressure to the work as you tighten the rod. You should cut some 2"–square pads from scrap pieces of 1/4" plywood to keep the metal tips from marring the face of your work.

The best results in joint–clamping come when you place the clamp's pressure points directly at the centerline of the work or joint to be glued. Snug-tightening is best, since over-tightening can damage the wood and, with gluing, force enough adhesive from the joint to cause uneven distribution and a weakened bond.

Sanding and Smoothing

A finish is only as good as the surface beneath it, and getting that surface just right takes a lot of time and a little bit of know-how. The kind of wood you use makes a difference, but the way you work it is just as important.

Before you begin sanding, take a look at the wood in a good light. It should be flat and the surface smooth before you can safely apply a

coating. Any glue runs or forced–out material should have been cleaned off with a damp cloth before they dried. If not, they can be trimmed off with a sharp chisel.

You should be aware that some manufactured wood pieces—moldings and trim especially—may be contaminated with silicone oils or waxes left there as cutter-head lubricants. These should be removed with a cloth soaked in mineral spirits, followed by an ammonia wash of one part clear ammonia to fifteen parts warm water, spread evenly over the entire surface, then wiped dry. Waxes and oils are usually OK with oil-based finishes, but can mottle water-based finishes and lacquers; that's why they must be removed before going any further.

Here's a quick lesson on sandpaper, or more properly, coated abrasive. It's made of tiny pieces of mineral grit glued onto some kind of backing. The grit determines how fast a paper will sand, and how much effort will be required to do it. The backing—and the glue or "binder" used to hold the grit in place—establishes how the sheet will stand up to wear and solvents.

There's not a whole lot to understanding how sandpaper works. The abrasive removes tool marks left in the surface of the wood and replaces them with grooves established by the size of the grit on the paper. Few large grooves are turned into many

Pipe clamps are especially useful when edge-gluing narrow bands.

GRIT CHART

Grade No.	Coarseness Rating
600	Super fine
500	
400	
360	Extra fine
320	
280	
240	Very fine
220	
180	
150	Fine
120	
100	
80	Medium
60	
50	
40	Coarse

A *belt sander can bring down rough wood quickly and easily.*

small grooves as a progressively finer grit size is used.

The terms "open coat" and "closed coat" are used to describe the amount of grit on the backing. An open coat has only about 50% to 70% of the surface covered with mineral. This has the effect of periodically declogging the paper, because the open spaces provide a place for the cuttings to lodge until they fall off. A closed coat is completely covered with sand, which offers a finer finish. In higher-grit (extra-fine) papers, the difference doesn't amount to much because the rough work has already been done. But with the lower-num-

bered grits, the open-style paper makes less heat and conserves material.

Grits can be either synthetic or natural. Though there are many different kinds of sandpaper, only a few are really practical for woodworking. Among the synthetic grits, aluminum oxide is the most common, and probably the one you'll use. It's light brown or white in color, and is ideal for general sanding and finishing work. For finishing by itself, another synthetic, silicon carbide, which is bright black, is generally recommended.

Garnet is a reddish mineral used a lot in sandpaper, even with the popularity of synthetics. It has the unique characteristic of breaking off as it works, presenting a new sharp facet with each fracture. Garnet paper does an excellent job but wears faster than the synthetics.

The backing used with sandpapers varies according to the tool the paper is going to be used on. Sheet papers and polyester cloth backings are both used, the latter more on belt sanders. For hand-held palm sanders, a paper backing with pressure-sensitive adhesive is common.

When sanding, always work from coarse to fine grits. You should begin with an 80 or 100 grit, and then progress to the next finer level, increasing the point range with each step. Using this rule, a grit progression of 80/120/220/400 would be typical.

Working with too heavy a grit size results in a lot of effort with no progress, because you're simply creating grooves. On the other hand, using too light a grit doesn't remove the deeper marks from the previous paper, so they'll eventually show up in the finish. Some softwoods don't require you to sand finer than 180 grit. The harder woods, however, may need to be taken down to a 400-grit or higher level. In general, a 220-grit sanding will give the best results, especially if you plan on using a water-based finish.

Besides the motor-driven palm sander, you might use a sanding block to achieve a flat surface and get a better feel for your work. You can also fold a paper sheet several times to do detail work or stiffen the paper in your fingers. Once you reach a 150-grit or finer level, you can begin sanding in any direction—not just with the grain—because the scratches you create will probably not be visible.

The most common error when using a palm sander is scrubbing it across the wood's surface too rapidly. You must remember that an oscillating sander is already moving at a rate of nearly 14,000 oscillations per minute, and you don't need to speed it up. Your hand with the sander in it should move about one inch per second to avoid leaving swirl marks in the surface.

Stock Preparation

Preparing your stock accurately can mean the difference between a casual hobby project and a really useful and attractive one. Wood that doesn't have square edges and straight, parallel surfaces to start with will display the same characteristics in the finished project.

Wood that's dressed carelessly produces ill-fitting joints and mismatches progressively down each step of assembly. But the machining of stock involves more than just running wood through some equipment. The normal routine is to first cut the boards to length, leaving a few inches extra for trimming. Then the stock should be jointed and planed, ripped to width, and finally cut to finished length.

Sometimes, the order of things is changed if there's a long piece of stock with an imperfection such as a cup or bow. In that case, it may need to be crosscut into shorter pieces—or ripped into individual strips—before it can be planed safely.

Once stock has been cut to rough length, it can be surfaced in the direction of the grain. Wood cut against the grain causes tearout and a produces a rough surface even after sanding.

The best way to determine grain direction is to first look at the curvature of the growth rings at the end of the board to establish which was the inside face, then—with that face up—the V-pattern that's visible points in the correct direction. On the opposite, or outside, face of the board, the correct direction is just the reverse.

Four feet, more or less, is the ideal length for jointing and planing, but exceptions must be made for components that are longer than that. Avoid machining short pieces less than 16".

- Face-jointing is using the jointer to remove high spots on the face of a board. When surfacing cupped or bowed stock, the concave side should rest on the table so the edges or ends touch first. These will be the first to be removed, until the board is uniformly flat.
- The thickness planer "reads" the board's one flat side and makes the opposite side parallel and uniform. Once the first side is planed, the board should be turned over and planed again, since the planer makes a smoother cut than a jointer. To maintain consistency, you should plane all your stock of the same thickness at one time before changing the machine's setting to make the next series of cuts.
- Edge-squaring is done on the jointer. If the board is crooked, the bad edge must be removed first. A hand plane can take off the high ends, but in severe cases the edge of the board must be cut. Snap a chalk line between the ends as a guide, then use a jigsaw to cut along the line. Square the jointer by checking its fence against the cutter head with a reliable square, then pass the stock through the machine with its edge hard against the table and its face hard against the fence.
- Ripping, or cutting to width, is done on the table saw. Always put the board's jointed edge against the fence to give the most accurate cut. On pieces that require accurate surfacing on all four sides, add 1/16" or so to the final edge to allow for jointing later.
- Final cutting for length is done on the table saw, or with a radial-arm saw. The initial cut squares one end, and the second cut establishes the finished length. On longer components, it may be impractical to rely on the short miter gauge to make an accurate final cut.

Chapter 5

choosing wood and materials

Wood is a perfect building material. It's strong but can still be worked with reliefs and pleasant shapes. It can be finished to show off its grain, or covered to hide its imperfections. And it's all around us in a variety of colors and species.

But wood can have its secrets to those who don't speak the language of the lumberyard. And the different wood species can be difficult to evaluate and identify without some guidance.

Certain kinds of wood are more suitable than others for certain tasks. The points covered in the next page or so will help you to make an informed decision, whether you're purchasing lumber from a retail yard, a home improvement center, or a mill supplier.

What About Species?

Trees are classified in two categories, hardwoods and softwoods. But don't rely just on the name, because a softwood like Douglas fir is actually harder than basswood, which is known as a hardwood.

Commercially available softwoods include pines, spruces, firs, and redwood. Hardwoods harvested for market include oak, birch, maple, cherry, and walnut. These woods are not only cut into strips and boards to sell, but are also sliced to face panels such as plywood, and are chipped up to manufacture fiberboard and particleboard.

All wood is made up of cellulose (the cell framework), lignin (the cement between the cells), organic extractives (which give the wood its color, density, scent, and rot resistance), and trace minerals.

Variations in these elements make the difference between hard and soft woods, stiff and flexible woods, and woods that are light or dark. The makeup of each species is fairly constant, so a wood's species has come to serve as a guideline in choosing wood for one purpose or another.

For general construction, softwoods are good because they're available, reasonably priced, and easy to work with. Most lumberyards or home improvement centers should have a dimensional lumber on hand for framing and finishing all the projects you'd want to build.

The hardwoods—used for cabinet and furniture manufacture—are more expensive and not as easy to come by, though some retail outlets supply them for home use. Hardwood is a bit more difficult to work with than softwood because it's more dense. That's compensated for to some degree by the fact that hardwoods offer a cleaner cut, are usually stronger, and have better appearance quality than softwoods in general.

Sizing and Dimensions

Lumber is sized and priced by its rough-sawn dimensions. But when the rough stock is planed for the market, the overall size can be reduced by 25% or more. The original sawn dimension is called its nominal size—after planing, the piece is sold by its actual dimension. This, if you've ever wondered, is why a 2 X 4 really measures only 1-1/2" by 3-1/2". A piece of lumber less than 1" thick and between 2" and 6" wide is called a strip. Stock less than 2" thick and up to 16" wide is a board. Dimension lumber measures from 2" to 4-1/2" thick and up to 16" wide. Standard lengths range from 6' to 16', in 2-foot increments.

Hardwoods are sized differently. Boards come in random widths up to 6", though wider boards can be custom-cut. Standard lengths run from

A 3/4" plywood panel with a cabinet-grade birch facing. The multiple veneer core helps to stiffen the material.

4' to 16'. Thickness is generally measured in 1/4" graduations, from 1" to 4", and is expressed as a fraction—for example, a 5/4" board measures 1-1/4" before it's planed.

Wood is sold commercially in volume by the board foot, a long-established standard by which each unit is equivalent to a rough board measuring 1" thick by 12" wide by 12" long, or 144 cubic inches of wood altogether. The rules are that any stock less than an inch thick is counted as a full inch, and anything over 1" is figured to the next larger 1/4".

In the market, 4 board feet could be a twelve-foot 1 X 4 or a 16-foot piece measuring 1-1/2" X 2". To calculate board feet, multiply thickness by width in inches, then multiply by length in feet and divide by 12.

Sheet and Panel Products

Solid lumber for both commercial and home use is steadily being supplanted by manufactured sheet goods. At one time, plywood was about the only panel product readily available, but today there are several kinds of panels that can be used to make good-looking and highly functional projects and furniture pieces.

Plywood—made of thin veneers glued so that the grain of adjacent layers run perpendicular to one another—comes in a standard 4' X 8' panel. There is a 3/16"-thick panel, then sizes run from 1/4" to 3/4" in 1/8" increments. The quality and cost of the board increases as more layers are used (regardless of finished thickness), because multiple layers improve the consistency and flatness of the sheets. Veneer plywood is stable and holds screws extremely well. It can be faced in a variety of wood types for finish and underlayment use.

Lumber-core plywood is a costly variant of its common cousin which isn't in general use. Its core stock is softwood or hardwood lumber rather than thin veneers, and although it stays flatter than regular plywood and has the same characteristics, it's really not worth the extra expense.

Medium-density fiberboard (MDF) is manufactured from small wood fibers bound together by resins with heat and pressure. It's less costly than either type of plywood and takes very well to cutting and routing. It also holds a screw nearly as well as plywood, though it does better with a sheet-metal thread–style fastener than with a regular wood screw and must use a pilot hole.

MDF is somewhat heavy and comes in sizes from 3/16" to over 1" in standard fractional dimensions. It's also made in 4' and 5' widths and in lengths up to 20'. One very attractive feature of these panels is that they can be ordered with a thin veneer of wood surface (these are called MDF-core plywood), which can be stained and finished like any other veneer. Otherwise, the unfinished panels, which are extremely smooth, can be covered with laminate or painted with excellent results. The main problem with MDF is that it's only beginning to become available on the retail market. Some outlets may stock it, and others may be able to order it in a manageable 4' X 8' size.

Particleboard is also called chipboard. It's made of small wood particles and fibers bonded in the same fashion as MDF. It comes either as a core sheet or as a plywood panel with a wood face and back. It's heavy but less expensive than any of the other sheets, and comes in the same standard sizes as medium-density fiberboard. Drawbacks? The sheets don't always cut cleanly and don't hold a fastener as well as the other products. On the other hand, particleboard is more readily available than MDF.

Lumber Grades

When a log is harvested, the lumber varies in quality. To assure that buyers get a product that's suited to their needs, the lumber is graded into standardized categories.

The grade is based on the size of the wood and the number and significance of defects (knots, pitch pockets, decay) that affect the strength, utility, or durability of the finished product. Hardwood and softwood are each graded further by use, which takes species, appearance, and structural integrity into account.

Softwood grades for construction fall into five different categories. No. 1 has tight knots and minor blemishes, and is used for finish work; No. 2 has larger knots and noticeable blemishes, and is suitable for paneling; No. 3 contains knotholes and visible flaws, fine for sheathing. Nos. 4 and 5 are low-quality boards.

Appearance lumber isn't graded for strength but has visual appeal for finish work. Select grades are described by letters and numbers: B & Btr (1 and 2 Clear) is a higher-quality product than C Select, which contains limited defects. D Select grade has minor surface imperfections.

Hardwood lumber is graded into categories, mainly for manufacturing. "Firsts and seconds" (FAS) is a combination of the two best grades—the boards must be at least 6" wide and 8' long. "Selects" are FAS-quality boards at least 4" wide and 6' in length.

Plywood panels can be made of softwood (Douglas fir, western hemlock, and pine) or hardwood (birch, oak, cherry, and walnut). The grades are established by the quality of the face and back veneers. The inspection stamps on the back of each panel show the grade of both sides, the wood species group number (lower numbers indicate stiffer panels), application for interior or exterior use, and the mill and testing marks.

Softwood panels are graded by letter: N—suitable for a natural finish and free of open defects; A—smooth and paintable, limited to 18 neatly made repairs; B—solid surfaced, with circular repair plugs and tight knots; C—knotholes up to 1" and tight knots to 1-1/2", with limited splits allowed.

Hardwood panels use number grades: 1-premium—book-matched grain with only minor defects; 1—good, but unmatched grain and minor defects; 2—sound, suitable for painting, with appearance defects and smooth patches.

Making the Best Choice

In lumberyard stock, the better grades will be free of major defects, but it's always a good idea to visually inspect the lumber you want before you buy it. Some places try to discourage "handpicking," but you shouldn't accept poor quality.

Things to be critical of in a piece of wood are knotholes, checks, wane (flat or rounded edges),`and warpage—either a bend or a twist in the wood. If appearance is a prime concern, as in hardwoods, stains or insect holes can affect your choice.

Workability is important, but with sharp-bladed tools problems can be reduced. A dense softwood such as Southern pine will cut and work well; hardwoods, especially oak, are tough on tool edges but have the same good qualities. The species to avoid are those that tear easily, are prone to split and warp, and give a ragged cut. The manufacturers of MDF panels recommend that table saws be equipped with sharp, all-purpose combination blades with high rake angles and a high tooth count (a minimum of 50 on a 10" blade).

DIMENSION LUMBER SIZES AND BOARD FOOTAGE

nominal size (inches)	actual size (inches)	board foot @ length in feet				
		8	10	12	14	16
1 X 2	3/4 X 1-1/2	1-1/3	1-2/3	2	2-1/3	2-2/3
1 X 3	3/4 X 2-1/2	2	2-1/2	3	3-1/2	4
1 X 4	3/4 X 3-1/2	2-2/3	3-1/3	4	4-2/3	5-1/3
1 X 6	3/4 X 5-1/2	4	5	6	7	8
1 X 8	3/4 X 7-1/4	5-1/3	6-2/3	8	9-1/3	10-2/3
1 X 10	3/4 X 9-1/4	6-2/3	8-1/3	10	11-2/3	13-1/3
1 X 12	3/4 X 11-1/4	8	10	12	14	14
2 X 4	1-1/2 X 3-1/2	5-1/3	6-2/3	8	9-1/3	10-2/3
2 X 6	1-1/2 X 5-1/2	8	10	12	14	16
2 X 8	1-1/2 X 7-1/4	10-2/3	13-1/3	16	18-2/3	21-1/3
2 X 10	1-1/2 X 9-1/4	13-1/3	16-2/3	20	23-1/3	26-2/3
2 X 12	1-1/2 X 11-1/4	16	20	24	28	32
4 X 4	3-1/2 X 3-1/2	10-2/3	13-1/3	16	18-2/3	21-1/3
4 X 6	3-1/2 X 5-1/2	16	20	24	28	32
6 X 6	5-1/2 X 5-1/2	24	30	36	42	48

Chapter 6

glues, screws, and hardware

Glues and Adhesives

It's not always possible to rely on glue alone to hold pieces of wood together, especially if the parts are in large sections or you're working with something substantial such as a cabinet or bed frame.

Nevertheless, glues, adhesives, and cements have their place in all kinds of wood construction, and can often be used alone or with the mechanical fasteners described further on in this chapter.

There are differences among the three kinds of bonding agents other than their names. Good old-fashioned glue is made from natural materials—animal by-products that have certain advantages over the newer ingredients used for the most part today. One of these, liquid hide glue, remains popular because it fills gaps easily, has a high initial tack, and has good strength characteristics as long as moisture isn't present. The other, casein glue, is processed from milk curd and mixed with water in the shop. It, like the liquid hide, dries slowly, so it's good for projects that take time to assemble. Unlike the hide glue, though, it's water resistant so can be used in more applications.

Adhesives are made from synthetics. The best all-around wood adhesive is aliphatic resin, a creamy yellow goo that comes already mixed in a bottle and is often referred to as "carpenters' glue." A variant of that is Type II adhesive, which is waterproof and specifically made for outdoor projects. Both these materials set up in 10 minutes or less, which means you have to work quickly with them. By the same token, their clamp time—the moments spent under pressure—can be as little as 60 minutes, though full-strength hardening takes about 24 hours.

Another adhesive often used for veneers and overlays, or when laminating (gluing together in layers), is urea formaldehyde, which comes as a powder then mixed with water, or in liquid form to which a dry powder hardener is added. It can be left open, or unclamped, for up to 30 minutes, but needs to stay under pressure for 6 to 12 hours while curing.

Cements are made from rubber suspended in a liquid vehicle. Contact cement is the most well known, and mainly used for holding veneers and plastic laminates in place on a wooden surface. It's spread with a brush or roller on

both surfaces and allowed to dry, then clamped precisely in place. Full curing occurs in a matter of hours, but the water-resistant bond takes place on contact.

It's worth taking the time to read the label on the product you're planning to use. Look for the set-up, or "open," time, for this will tell you how many minutes you have available to fiddle with fit and placement before the glue begins to set. The clamp time mentioned previously also affects your work because you'll want to know how long you'll need to keep your clamps in place before they can be used elsewhere. Be aware that curing time can be affected by temperature, which speeds up the drying process; most agents require ambient temperatures to be over 65 or 70 degrees Fahrenheit in order to bond properly. To be on the safe side, glue joints should be allowed to dry 24 hours before attempting to cut or rout them.

For the best glue joint, the stock should be joined as soon as possible after it's cut, and the parts should fit well together, without showing any large gaps. Grease, oil, and wax diminish the strength of a joint, so the wood surfaces need to be free of any film from saw blades or finishes. A slightly rough surface makes for a good bond.

When clamping, do not overtighten the joint because it will force adhesive from the union. This will

weaken the bond and probably cause some leakage which can stain the wood or pose a problem in finishing. Any excess adhesive should be wiped immediately from the outside surface of the wood with a damp cloth (contact cement can be removed with solvent, but it tends to "string" rather than run, so it's not really a problem to work with).

Screws and Fasteners

Fasteners are used to join wooden parts and attach hardware such as knobs and hinges. They include nails, brads, screws, and lag bolts.

Nails vary in length and thickness. As the nail increases in length, so does its diameter. Penny sizes—indicated by the letter "d"—are a traditional unit of English measurement based on weight, which has evolved today into a standard based on length. Hence, all nails of a particular penny size are the same length, but the diameters vary from one type of nail to another. Penny sizes range from 2d (1") to 60d (6") in length.

Casing and finish nails have set heads designed to hold the wood from beneath the surface, allowing the hole to be covered if needed. The casing nail is similar to a finish nail, but with a more conical-shaped head to allow it to grip the wood with more effect. Both these nails are driven the last blow or two with a nail set, or a pointed punch described further in the chapter on tools. They can be used to secure panels and trim on most furnture projects.

Brads, or wire nails, are smaller and most often used to hold strips and trim. These finer nails have diameters measured by wire gauge, ranging from a 19g to 12g. In "gauge talk," the higher number indicates a thinner nail, a 19-gauge brad having only a .042" diameter. Brads and wire nails are measured by actual length in inches rather than by the penny size.

Wood screws come in a variety of styles, finishes, and materials, but only a few need to be mentioned here. Flathead Phillips-drive screws or the popular taper-headed cabinet screws are common and easy to work with. Some are pointed and coated for self-boring and others are designed with tiny cutting edges to countersink themselves. Square-drive screws with four-sided drive sockets can be bought in lots, but you'll need a special—and fortunately not cost-ly—drive bit to install and remove them. These are positive-grip heads that won't slip even under tough conditions.

The traditional slotted flathead screw has almost been replaced by these newer styles, but maybe for good reason. They don't hold a screw-driver blade well and for the most part must be hand-driven. Save them for those special occasions when you need that old-fashioned look.

Wood screws are sized by gauge number, which indicates their diam-eter in inches at the body, just below the head. They come in lengths from 3/8" to 3-1/2", though extended lengths of up to 6" are available for special purposes. For example, a No. 8 X 1-1/2" screw is one that's 5/32" in diameter and 1-1/2" long (see the chart below for a full range of dimensions).

A screw's thread design is worth considering, though it's not neces-sarily a critical factor. Manufacturers may offer screws made with a fine pitch (or less distance between the threads)—to secure hardwoods—or a coarse one to grip softwoods.

Standard wood screws will usu-ally work with particleboard and fiberboard, but straight-shank (non tapered) screws with widely spaced threads and a narrow core diameter have been specially developed for these manufactured sheet materials.

Lag screws are large-diameter square- or hex-head steel fasteners with shank sizes from 1/4" to 1/2". Lengths range from 1" to 6" or 8". These are largely decorative, or used when a screw larger than No. 12 is needed. For more positive holding power, a machine screw or carriage bolt is a better choice because it uses a nut and washer to secure the joint from both sides.

Finally, there are the odds-and-ends fasteners for specific purposes: screw hooks, cup hangers, shoulder

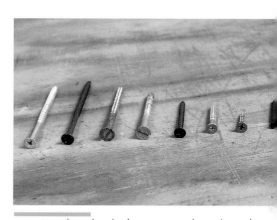

A *variety of wood and cabinet screws. The traditional wood screws like those in the center have larger shank diameters.*

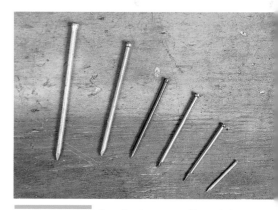

Finish and wire nails, or brads, are usually set below the surface with a nailset and covered with filler.

A small butt hinge with fixed pin.

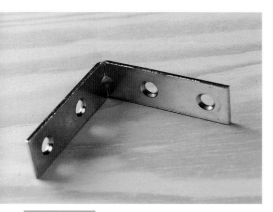

Corner braces are usually used to hold corners from the inside.

hooks, and screw eyes. These are usually brass plated and under 3" in length, with diameters measured in the wire-gauge scale. For heavier jobs, longer, bright-plated hooks and hangers are available. Shoulder hooks and cup hangers have a shoulder or stop where the threads meet the shank.

Hardware

Hardware includes the miscellaneous metal fixtures used in finishing a project—hinges, brackets, latches, drawer slides, handles, and knobs (even wooden ones).

Hinge hardware can be a bit confusing because of the terminology. Butt hinge is the generic term for the two-leaf square or rectangular fixture joined in the middle by knuckles that pivot on a pin. More recently, the concealed hinge—a European-style piece of hardware that mounts from the inside—has been replacing the butt hinge, especially on cabinets that don't use face frames or wide borders around the doors.

It's important, however, to look a bit further. There is a full-mortise hinge (made to be set into recesses, or mortises, cut into the surface of the wood); a half-mortise hinge (one leaf is mortised into the door and the other is simply screwed to the jamb surface); a full-surface hinge (both hinge leaves are fixed to the surface);

and a half-surface hinge (one leaf is attached to the door's surface and the other is mortised into the jamb).

And the European hinges offer other choices to think about: Because they use extended arms in addition to simple knuckles, they can be designed to swing clear of an opening, or open up to 270° for unobstructed access. They can also be self-closing.

The design of the project makes a difference too. With a cabinet, the doors can be full overlay, where they completely cover the face edge of a cabinet's side or carcase; half overlay, in which two doors share and cover a common jamb (as in the middle of a row of cabinets); or inset, where the door is recessed into the cabinet carcase to create a flush surface, and the cabinet's face edge is exposed.

It's also common to have 3/4"-thick doors that are lipped at the perimeter by incorporating a 3/8" X 3/8" rabbet, or relief, into the back edges. These doors use hinges with leaves that are bent at multiple right angles to conform to the relief in the wood. These hinges are usually described as inset because the butt or "hanging" leaf is bent to the inside; offset hinges are those in which the leaves are formed away from the center of the pin.

Brackets are used to help support shelves and reinforce corners. In the days when furniture construction used wood almost exclusively, corner braces—made of triangular blocks of wood—provided this support. Today, it's quicker and easier to let shaped metal do the job.

Corner braces come in a variety of styles—in metal and nylon—to secure corners from the inside. Corner plates, in the shape of an "L," hold corners from the edge of the wood or on a flush surface when pieces are perpendicular.

Latches and catches can be mechanical or magnetic. Externally mounted turn catches and bolts are obvious in that they hook or slip into a socket or retainer mounted on the framework. Internal catches are usually smaller, less conspicuous, and often quite clever in their function. Besides the common bullet and double-roller or spring catch, there are touch-latch types that release when the door is pressed in, and flush-mounted ring-pull styles that unlatch by lifting a central ring.

Drawer slides are ready-made tracks that fit between the cabinet carcase and the sides of the drawers themselves. The rail section mounts to the cabinet and the slide arm fastens to the drawer. Nylon or steel ball bearings allow the arm to glide in and out.

Most small or lightweight drawers don't need slides at all, because they can be fit loosely enough to function without binding. But when a drawer gets heavy, or wide and awkward, it needs positive guidance. The two things most important in selecting drawer slides are length (they can't be any longer in closed position than the drawer itself) and weight capacity (a 25–to 150–pound range is common).

Handles and knobs are a matter of design and cost, unless they're part of the latch. Most knobs and pulls are surface-mounted from the front, or blind-mounted from the rear using screws passed through holes in the door and drawer faces.

The European-style hinge is surface-mounted inside or can be mortised in.

A surface-mounted cabinet hinge for a half-overlay door.

SCREW CHART

size or gauge no.	4	6	8	10	12
shank diameter	7/64"	9/64"	5/32"	3/16"	7/32"
lengths (by 1/4s)	3/8"-1"	1/2"-2"	1/2"-3"	3/4"-3-1/2"	3/4"-3-1/2"
shank hole drill	1/8"	9/64"	11/64"	3/16"	7/32"
pilot hole drill	1/16"	5/64"	3/32"	7/64"	1/8"

Chapter 7

fixes and finishes

A finish does a number of things. It protects the wood from stains and wear, preserves it from the effects of sunlight and moisture if it's exposed, enhances it to bring out color and grain patterns, and can even alter it by hiding defects or adding color. It does all this by covering the wood with a thin film of resin, made workable with the addition of a solvent which evaporates during drying.

There are essentially two kinds of finishes: "evaporative" and "reactive." The difference between the two is that evaporative finishes start as a flowable resin and dry as a hardened resin; only the solvent has evaporated. This is not so with reactive finishes, which undergo a chemical change as the film is formed to become an entirely different material.

As far as you are concerned, the difference means two things. First, evaporative finishes can be re-dissolved once they've dried by introducing the original solvent. This is what happens every time a new coat is applied, and when it's dry, the finished film becomes one single layer. (A reactive finish, on the other hand, dries in separate layers.) Secondly, evaporative finishes, because of their tendency to self-meld, are a lot easier to maintain because repairs on them generally don't show.

What's the best choice? Among the evaporatives (which include the time-tested shellacs and lacquers), an easy-to-work-with water-based polyurethane varnish, sold as a polyurethane coating, is at the top of the list. For reactive finishes, polyurethane varnish in an oil base offers the benefits of hardness, adhesion, flexibility, and water-resistance. And though it doesn't do well over time in direct sunlight, it can be applied easily over stains and existing finishes.

For outdoor things or those in transitionary use, you might consider a clear wood finish, either oil-based or water-borne, such as the kind used on decks and railings. A semitransparent stain also works well in this kind of application because it brings up the natural features of the wood beneath and protects the grain by soaking in and providing some ultraviolet shield in the form of pigmentation.

Since most of the projects in this book are for the indoors, you will probably be considering paint as an option. Enamel paint can provide a smooth, hard, colorful finish that

fends off moisture and protects the wood from scuffs and the effects of direct sunlight. For some of the projects, the way paint is applied can highlight certain features and mute others. Decorative treatments can also be painted right on a panel surface to make it functionally attractive.

In softwoods or wood products that have a tendency to absorb a finish, a sanding sealer should be used to prepare the wood before applying paint or stain. Usually, a single coat will be sufficient, and giving the wood a light sanding after it's applied will bring down any raised grain.

If you plan on staining the wood to bring out its natural characteristics, you'll have to do that before applying whatever protective finish you choose. There is a confusing array of stains available, and to make matters more confusing, there are colorants such as Japan colors (made with linseed oil), universal tinting colors (pastes that are harmonious with almost any coating), and pigment powders used for touch-up work and making special putties and stains.

But to simplify things, stains can be categorized as either pigment stains or dye stains. The difference is that pigments are mineral particles in suspension within the stain that settle in the pores of the wood and on its surface. Dyes are crystals that are in solution within the stain and only color the wood in a very trans-

parent way. So pigmented stains will enhance the existing grain pattern in a piece of wood, and will even make the surface muddy if applied too thickly. Dyes don't have that capability, and are able to color without hiding—or improving—the wood's natural characteristics.

When applying pigmented stains such as wiping stains or pigmented oil or water stains, flood the surface then wipe it off with a rag or sponge. The more you leave on the wood, the darker it will turn out. Don't restain until the first coast has dried.

With dyes, like penetrating oil stains or penetrating dyes, the process is similar, but the amount left on doesn't affect color; that's done by either adding powder to darken it or adding more solvent to lighten it. Color mixing can be done beforehand or in a later application once the first one has dried.

how to cut a half-lap joint

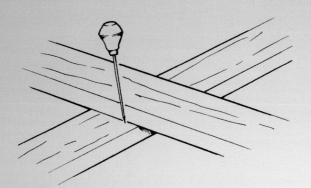

✏️ **step 1.** Place the two pieces together where you want the joint. Mark along each side of the joint on both pieces with an awl or pencil.

✏️ **step 2.** Mark the depth halfway on each piece using a marking gauge, and score the midpoint lines with the gauge's spur. Connect the face lines with the midpoint lines by marking along the gauge's beam or using a try square to carry the lines around.

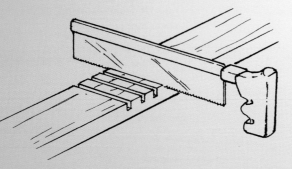

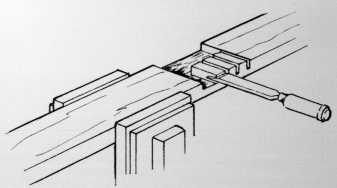

✏️ **step 3.** Use a backsaw or tenon saw to make shoulder cuts to the depth mark along each side. Then make a series of center cuts between the shoulder cuts, all to the same depth.

✏️ **step 4.** Slice away the waste material from each piece with a sharp chisel, working from the sides toward the center. Level the center by paring the wood, holding the chisel flat. Dry-fit the two components before joining them.

Projects

side rack

Here's a contemporary open shelf for holding dishes, cups, utensils, and what-have-you in the kitchen. Its strong hardwood frame hangs on securely mounted wall fasteners and can easily be moved if needed. The rack is over 4' in length, but building it longer or shorter is no problem at all because of the repeating dowel pattern.

Suggested Tools

Table saw

Dado blade

Coping saw

3/8" Drill

1/2" Forstner bit

No. 8 screw bit

Phillips-head driver bit

Try square

Tape measure

Pipe clamps

1/4" Chisel

Hammer

Nail set

Hardware and Supplies

9-Gauge X 1-1/2" shoulder hooks

Flush hangers

Aliphatic resin glue

No. 8 X 1-1/4" wood screws

No. 8 X 1-1/2" wood screws

No. 8 X 2" wood screws

16-Gauge X 1-1/4" brads

Wood filler

Polyurethane

Cut List

Oak or birch is recommended for this project.

2	Top rails	3/4" X 1-1/2" X 52-1/2"
2	Bottom rails	3/4" X 1-1/2" X 52-1/2"
2	Sides	3/4" X 1-1/2" X 12"
2	Sides	3/4" X 1-1/2" X 11-5/8"
18	Dowels	1/2" X 18"
7	Stretchers	3/4" X 1-1/2" X 9-3/4"
2	Face boards	1/2" X 1-3/4" X 56"
1	Shelf (plywood)	3/8" X 9" X 53"

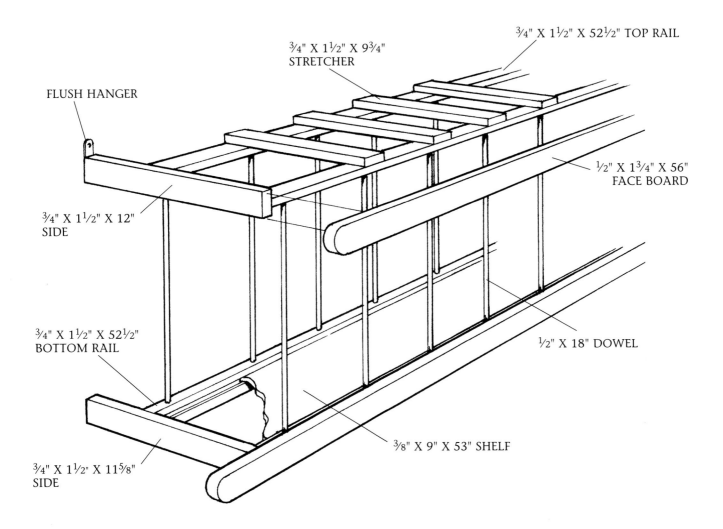

¾" X 1½" X 52½" TOP RAIL

¾" X 1½" X 9¾"
STRETCHER

FLUSH HANGER

½" X 1¾" X 56"
FACE BOARD

¾" X 1½" X 12"
SIDE

¾" X 1½" X 52½"
BOTTOM RAIL

½" X 18" DOWEL

¾" X 1½" X 11⅝"
SIDE

⅜" X 9" X 53" SHELF

Construction Procedures

1. Using a table saw, rip all the 1-1/2" stock to width if needed. Cut the top and bottom rails, the sides, and the stretchers to the lengths indicated.

2. Cut a 3/8" X 3/8" dado into the face of each bottom rail, down the center. Mark a point 3" from one end of the two 11-5/8" side pieces and cut similar dadoes from those points to the ends of the boards, down the center of each face. Clean and square the stopped end of the dadoes with a chisel.

3. Mark nine points 6" apart and centered down the narrow edge of each bottom rail, and the face of each top rail, beginning at a point 2-1/4" from one end. Use a 1/2" Forstner bit to drill 3/8"-deep sockets at each of these points. Glue the 18 1/2" X 18" dowels into the sockets, making certain the dadoes on the bottom rails are facing each other.

4. Fasten one 12" side piece to each of the top rails so that the forward rail is flush with the end, and the rear edge of the back rail is 2-1/4" from the opposite end. The lower edge of each side should be flush with the bottom of each top rail. Fasten with No. 8 X 1-1/2" wood screws countersunk into the side pieces.

5. Cut the 3/8" plywood shelf to the dimensions indicated. Then slip it between the bottom rails into the dadoes. Fasten one 11-5/8" side piece to each of the bottom rails so that the forward ends are flush with the front rail's face and the back rail is centered 2-1/4" from the opposite end.

6. Mark seven points 6-1/2" apart on the upper faces of the top rails starting from one end. Center one stretcher at each of these points, drill, and fasten with glue and one No. 8 X 1-1/4" wood screw per joint.

7. Rip the 1/2" face boards to 1-3/4" in width and cut them to 56" in length. Round the ends with a coping saw to roughly a 7/8" radius. Fasten the face boards to the front of the top and bottom rails so there's a 1/4" downward overhang from the top, and one 1/4" upward from the bottom. Use 1-1/4" brads set below the surface.

8. Sand the wood and finish the project with stain (if needed) and polyurethane.

9. Fasten flush hangers to the wall end of the upper side pieces with No. 8 X 1/4" wood screws. Use No. 8 X 2" screws to fasten the hangers to the wall studs. Attach the shoulder hooks to the face boards as desired.

worktable

With a 30-inch-square work surface, two storage areas, and four full-length drawers accessible from two sides, this work station on wheels makes a useful addition to any kitchen. Topped with any manufactured synthetic counter material, the table is sturdy enough for any pounding or chopping chores you may encounter.

Suggested Tools

Table saw

Dado blade

3/8" Drill

5/16" Drill bit

3/8" Drill bit

1/2" Drill bit

No. 6 screw bit

Phillips-head driver bit

Router

1/2" Straight bit

1/2" Chisel

Try square

Coping saw

Marking gauge

Tape measure

Pipe clamps

Hammer

Nail set

Cut List

Oak, birch, or maple, A-C plywood, and white pine are recommended for this project.

2	Rails	1" X 1-1/2" X 21"
2	Sides	1" X 1-1/2" X 9-3/4"
12	Slats	1/2" X 1-1/2" X 10-1/4"
4	Stands	1-1/2" X 1-1/2" X 12"
4	Legs	2" X 2" X 32-1/2"
1	Countertop (synthetic)	3/4" X 30-1/4" X 30-1/4"
2	Skirt	3/4" X 4-1/2" X 25-1/4"
1	Drawer shelf (plywood)	3/4" X 25-1/4" X 28-3/4"
8	Drawer faces	3/4" X 3-5/8" X 6"
8	Drawer sides	1/2" X 3-1/2" X 27-1/4"
4	Drawer bottoms	1/2" X 4-3/4" X 27-1/4"
4	Steel cross dowels	5/16" X 3"
4	Corner braces	1/2" X 1"
2	Rails	1" X 1-1/2" X 23-3/4"
2	Rails	1" X 1-1/2" X 26-3/4"
13	Slats	1/2" X 1-3/4" X 24-3/4"

Hardware and Supplies

No. 6 X 1-1/2" cabinet screws

No. 6 X 2-1/4" cabinet screws

5/16" X 3" Steel cross dowels

1/2" X 1" Corner brackets

1-1/2" Finish nails

16-Gauge X 1-1/4" brads

3/8" Dowel

1" Knobs

14" Towel bar

2" X 2-3/4" Brake casters

Aliphatic resin glue

Wood filler

Wash or pigmented stain

Polyurethane

Construction Procedure

1. Cut the rails, sides, and slats of the small rack to the dimensions indicated in the cut list. Then cut the four 12" stands to size.

2. Use a dado blade to cut a 1/2" X 1/2"-deep, full-length slot down the center of the 1" face of each rail. Measure down 1/4" from the top of each stand and cut 1" X 1/4"-deep slots into the two inside corner faces of each.

3. Mark a point in the center of each slot and drill a 3/4"- deep 3/8" hole. Mark and drill matching 3/8" holes into the ends of the rail and side pieces. Cut eight 3/8" X 1-1/8" dowels, and use glue to make two assemblies, each consisting of a rail and two stands. Clamp until dry. Glue and fit the remaining four dowels into the side holes.

4. Glue the two side pieces onto the dowels on one of the rail assemblies and fit them firmly into the slots. Place the 12 slats into the rail dado, then carefully fit and glue the other rail assembly into place on the ends of the side pieces with the slats in its dado. Clamp until dry.

5. Cut the plywood drawer shelf to size. Measure 1" in from the sides along each 28-3/4" edge and drill 1/2"-diameter holes 1/2" from the

edge through the shelf. Then drill 5/16" holes from the edges to meet the 1/2" holes. Press in the steel dowel connector nuts.

6. Cut the four legs to size. Measure down 4-1/4" from the top of each leg and mark one face with a point in the center. Drill a 5/16" hole horizontally through each leg at that point. On the opposing inside faces, cut 1/4"-deep, 3/4" X 4-1/2" rabbets for the skirts into the rear corners, using a 1/2" straight bit in the router. Square the ends with a chisel. Then use the steel dowels to attach the legs to the shelf by threading them through the legs and into the connector nuts in the shelf.

7. Fasten the corner brackets adjacent to each skirt rabbet so their tops are even with the top of each leg. Use the hardware provided to screw the brackets to the legs. Fit the countertop temporarily in place and mark from the underside where the bracket fasteners should go. Drill mounting holes into the bottom surface no deeper than 5/8".

8. Cut the two skirts to the sizes shown. Stain them at this point if you want them set off with a different color. Slip the skirts into place from the top of the legs, and glue and nail each skirt to the 28-3/4" edge of the drawer shelf so the bot-

toms are flush with the lower face of the shelf. Place the countertop back in position and fasten from the bottom with the screws provided. They cannot be any longer than 3/4".

9. Cut the rails of the lower shelf to the two lengths indicated. On the 26-3/4" set, use a coping saw to cut 1" X 1" notches from each corner. Cut a 1/2" X 1/2" dado down the center of the 1" face of each 23-3/4" rail. Assemble the frame temporarily and use a No. 6 screw bit to drill holes through the notch tips and into the ends of the shorter rail pieces.

10. Cut the 13 slats to the sizes shown. Stain them now if you plan to. Fit them into the rail dadoes and fasten the two end rails to the dadoed rails using glue and No. 6 X 1-1/2" screws. Measure down 11" from the bottom of the drawer shelf and fasten the lower rack at that point by using a No. 6 screw bit to drill holes obliquely from the lower corners of the rack into the legs. Fasten with glue and No. 6 X 2-1/4" screws.

11. Cut the drawer bottoms, sides, and faces to the sizes indicated. Glue and nail the drawer sides to the bottoms with 16- gauge X 1-1/4" wire brads. Set the heads with a nail set. Glue the faces directly to the ends of the drawer cases and fasten with 1-1/4" brads. Set the heads, then fill the holes with wood filler.

12. Sand and finish the wood with polyurethane. Center and install the towel bar, the casters, and the drawer knobs once the finish has dried.

Tighten the four steel dowels firmly. The small rack is movable and does not get fastened to the work surface.

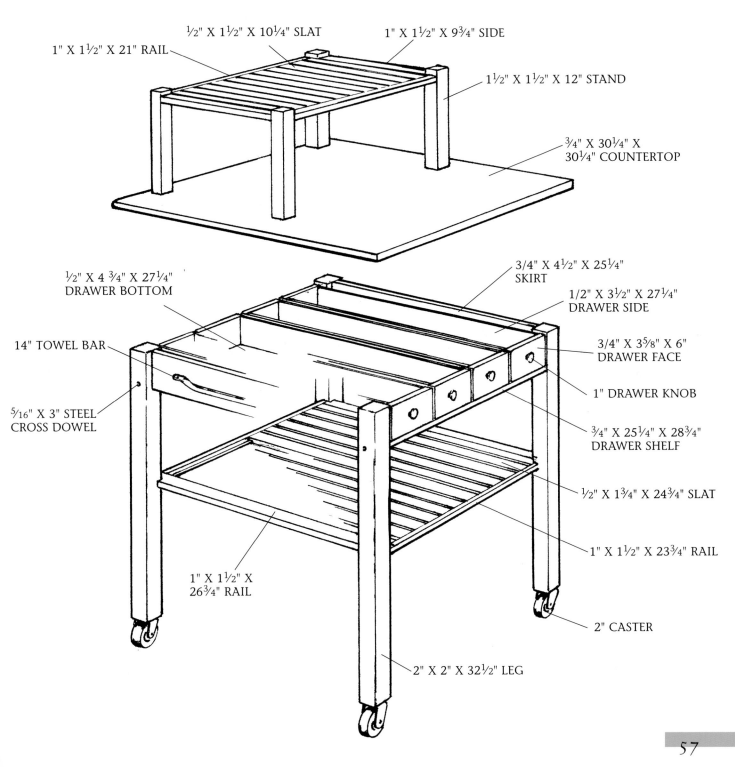

½" X 1½" X 10¼" SLAT

1" X 1½" X 9¾" SIDE

1" X 1½" X 21" RAIL

1½" X 1½" X 12" STAND

¾" X 30¼" X 30¼" COUNTERTOP

3/4" X 4½" X 25¼" SKIRT

½" X 4 ¾" X 27¼" DRAWER BOTTOM

1/2" X 3½" X 27¼" DRAWER SIDE

14" TOWEL BAR

3/4" X 3⁵⁄₈" X 6" DRAWER FACE

1" DRAWER KNOB

⁵⁄₁₆" X 3" STEEL CROSS DOWEL

¾" X 25¼" X 28¾" DRAWER SHELF

½" X 1¾" X 24¾" SLAT

1" X 1½" X 23¾" RAIL

1" X 1½" X 26¾" RAIL

2" CASTER

2" X 2" X 32½" LEG

57

cup hanger

If you can fasten a board to a wall, you've already completed half of this simple project. Bristling with hooks, the pair of boards has a comfortably narrow profile, spans just over a 5-foot section of wall, and holds 14 cups.

Suggested Tools

Table saw
Backsaw
Miter box
3/8" Drill
1/8" Drill bit
1/16" Drill bit
Router
3/8" Cove bit
Hammer
Tape measure

Hardware and Supplies

No. 6 X 2-1/2" cabinet screws
16-Gauge X 1-1/4" brads
11-Gauge X 1-1/2" cup hooks
1-5/16" Flush hangers
Aliphatic resin glue
Dark stain
Polyurethane

Construction Procedure

1. Rip the back pieces to width and cut both to length.

2. Cut a 45-degree miter into one end of the upper molding piece. Measure 67-1/2" from the outside, or front, edge and cut a second 45-degree miter. Repeat with lower molding, but cut to a 66-3/4" length. Cut the upper and lower end moldings to fit, using the dimensions indicated as a guide.

Cut List

Clear pine or maple is recommended for this project.

1	Back	3/4" X 5-1/2" X 66"
1	Upper molding	3/4" X 2" X 67-1/2"
2	Upper end molding	3/4" X 2" X 2"
1	Lower molding	3/4" X 1" X 66-3/4"
2	Lower end molding	3/4" X 1" X 1-1/2"
2	End molding	1/4" X 3/4" X 6"
1	Back	3/4" X 3" X 42"

3. Using a 3/8" cove bit, profile the edges of the smaller back board. Stain and finish both pieces.

4. Predrill holes about 12" apart and fasten both moldings to the back board with 16-gauge X 1-1/4" brads. Set the heads. Glue and fasten the upper and lower end moldings in the same manner. Then trim and fasten the two 6" end moldings. Finish all trim with polyurethane.

5. Drill eight 1/8" holes 9-1/8" apart down the center of the longer back piece. Then drill six 1/8" holes 6" apart down the center of the smaller back piece. Install the cup hooks.

6. Mount the larger rack to the wall using three no. 6 x 2-1/2" screws. Attach two flush hangers to the back of the smaller rack and hang from picture hangers.

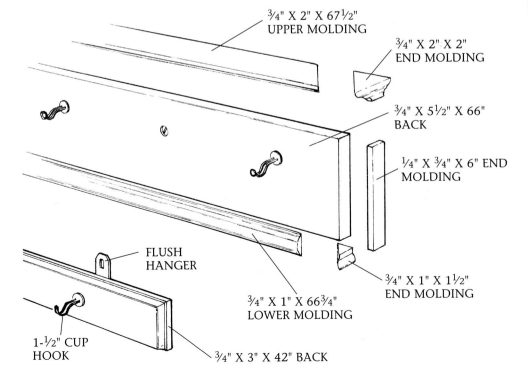

¾" X 2" X 67½"
UPPER MOLDING

¾" X 2" X 2"
END MOLDING

¾" X 5½" X 66"
BACK

¼" X ¾" X 6" END
MOLDING

¾" X 1" X 1½"
END MOLDING

¾" X 1" X 66¾"
LOWER MOLDING

FLUSH
HANGER

1-½" CUP
HOOK

¾" X 3" X 42" BACK

hideaway spice cabinet

A spice cabinet and kitchen workstation all in one, this compact case fits neatly and unobtrusively against the wall, taking up only about 6" of depth on the counter. Once opened, the cabinet reveals racks for spices and condiments and a place for utensils. The left-side door opens to become a cutting board.

Cut List

White pine or A-C interior plywood is recommended for this project.

2	Frames	3/4" X 5-1/2" X 34"
2	Sides	3/4" X 5-1/2" X 17-1/4"
1	Divider	3/4" X 4-1/2" X 17-1/4"
1	Base spacer	3/4" X 5-1/4" X 16-1/4"
2	Face trim	1/4" X 1-1/2" X 18-3/4"
2	Face trim	1/4" X 1-1/2" X 34"
1	Back (hardboard)	1/4" X 17" X 33-1/2"
1	Utensil door (MDF)	3/4" X 15-3/8" X 15-5/8"
1	Cutting board	1/2" X 14" X 15"
1	Trim rail	1-1/4" X 1-1/2" X 15-3/8"
1	Spice door	3/4" X 15-3/8" X 15-5/8"
2	Door shelves	3/4" X 2" X 12-7/8"
2	Sides	3/4" X 2-1/2" X 15-5/8"
2	Frame	3/4" X 2-1/2" X 12-7/8"
3	Shelf rod	1/4" X 13-3/8"
1	Hinge strip	3/4" X 1-1/2" X 15-5/8"
2	Cabinet shelves	3/4" X 2" X 15-1/2"

Suggested Tools

Table saw

Dado blade

Backsaw

Miter box

3/8" Drill

No. 6 screw bit

1/16" Drill bit

1/4" Drill bit

Phillips-head driver bit

1/2" Chisel

Try square

Tape measure

Hammer

Nail set

Hardware and Supplies

Magnetic utensil bars

No. 6 X 1-1/4" cabinet screws

No. 6 X 1-1/2" cabinet screws

No. 6 X 2-1/4" roundhead brass screws

No. 6 X 1-1/4" roundhead brass screws

16-Gauge X 1" finish nails

16-Gauge X 1-1/2" finish nails

9-Gauge X 1-1/2" cup hook

1-1/4" X 15-1/2" Piano hinges

Magnetic catch

1-1/4" Porcelain knob

Aliphatic resin

Wood filler

Latex paint

Construction Procedure

1. Cut the sides, frames, divider, and base spacer to the sizes indicated in the cut list. Cut a 1/4"-deep, 1/2"-wide rabbet with the table saw into the edges of the two frame and two side pieces. Stop the dado cuts on the frame pieces about 3/4" from the ends and complete the cuts to within 1/4" of the edges with a chisel.

2. Butt the top and bottom frame pieces against the side pieces and drill two countersunk holes at each joint using a No. 6 screw bit. Fasten the corners together with glue and No. 6 X 1-1/2" screws.

3. Measure 16-5/8" from the left inside of this cabinet frame and make a mark at the top and bottom frame pieces. Center the vertical divider at these points with the back edge flush to the shoulder of the dadoes. Fasten from the top and bottom with countersunk No. 6 X 1-1/2" screws.

4. Glue the base spacer to the lower frame piece on the inside of the left half of the cabinet. Fasten from the bottom with No. 6 X 1-1/4" cabinet screws. Cut and glue the hinge strip to the inside of the cabinet's right side, flush with the forward edge.

5. Cut the cabinet shelves to the sizes indicated. Fasten them 5" apart, through the divider and the side piece using countersunk No. 6 X 1-1/4" cabinet screws.

6. Cut the hardboard back to size and tack it into the dado rebate at the back of the frame using 16-gauge X 1" finish nails.

7. Cut the door frames, shelves, and side pieces to the sizes indicated. Drill 1/4"-deep, 1/4" holes into the inside faces of the sides at points 4-1/2", 9-1/2", and 13-3/8" from the top edges and 1/2" from the front edge. Butt the sides against the frame and shelf pieces with the shelves 6" and 11" from the upper ends of the sides, and all horizontal members recessed from its forward edge. The rods should be installed in their sockets before fastening the shelves. Fasten the shelves and frames through the sides with countersunk No. 6 X 1-1/4" cabinet screws, using two screws per joint.

8. Cut the spice door to size and fasten it to the door frame using glue and 16-gauge X 1-1/2" finish nails set beneath the surface. The door panel should be flush at the right side with a 1" overhang at the left.

9. Fasten one of the 15-1/2" piano hinges to the hinge strip and the right side of the spice door assembly using the hardware provided. Make sure the door is centered in the opening, without binding, before fastening the screws.

10. Cut the utensil door to the size indicated. Trim the rail handle to length and place it 2" below one of the 15-3/8" edges, which will be the top edge. Position the cutting board over the inside surface of the door and use a No. 6 screw bit to drill holes at each corner, the two lower ones 1-1/4" deep and the upper ones 2-1/4" in depth to penetrate the back of the handle. Install the screws.

11. Fasten the lower edge of the utensil door to the base spacer with the remaining 15-1/2" piano hinge, using the hardware provided. A magnetic catch may be used to hold the top of the door closed.

12. Miter-cut the two side trim pieces to length and tack them in place with 1" finish nails set beneath the surface. Fit the two horizontal trim pieces and cut them as needed. Nail in place.

13. Fill all the nail and screw holes as needed. Sand and seal the cabinet, and paint it as desired. Install the magnetic utensil bars and the cup hook, and fasten the 1-1/4" knob to the spice door. Secure the cabinet to the wall from the back.

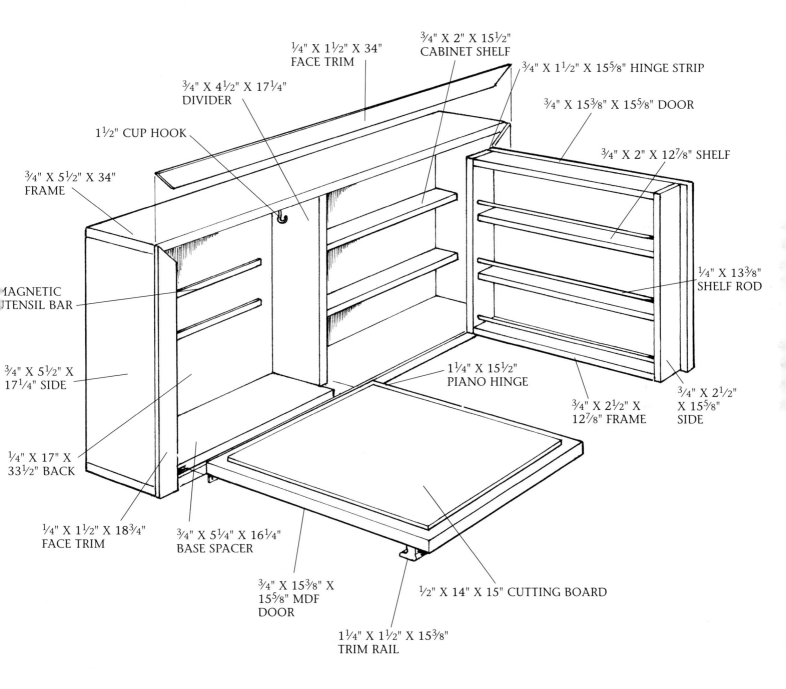

¼" X 1½" X 34"
FACE TRIM

¾" X 2" X 15½"
CABINET SHELF

¾" X 4½" X 17¼"
DIVIDER

¾" X 1½" X 15⅝" HINGE STRIP

¾" X 15⅜" X 15⅝" DOOR

1½" CUP HOOK

¾" X 2" X 12⅞" SHELF

¾" X 5½" X 34"
FRAME

MAGNETIC
UTENSIL BAR

¼" X 13⅜"
SHELF ROD

¾" X 5½" X
17¼" SIDE

1¼" X 15½"
PIANO HINGE

¾" X 2½" X
12⅞" FRAME

¾" X 2½"
X 15⅝"
SIDE

¼" X 17" X
33½" BACK

¼" X 1½" X 18¾"
FACE TRIM

¾" X 5¼" X 16¼"
BASE SPACER

¾" X 15⅜" X
15⅝" MDF
DOOR

½" X 14" X 15" CUTTING BOARD

1¼" X 1½" X 15⅜"
TRIM RAIL

63

corner cabinet

Everyone has a corner somewhere that could be put to better use. This cabinet, between a kitchen and dining room, fills a space that might otherwise be collecting dust. It has six functional shelves enclosed in a cohesive pine frame.

Suggested Tools

Table saw

Coping saw

3/8" Drill

3/8" Drill bit

No. 6 screw bit

Phillips-head driver bit

1/2" Chisel

Try square

Tape measure

Marking gauge

Protractor

Pipe clamps

Hammer

Nail set

Hardware and Supplies

No. 6 X 1-1/2" cabinet screws

16-Gauge X 1" brads

16-Gauge X 1-1/2" finish nails

18-Gauge X 1" brads

3/8" Dowel

1" Knobs

1-1/4" X 2" Butt hinges

Magnetic catches

Aliphatic resin glue

Wood filler

Cut List

Pine or poplar and A-C interior plywood are recommended for this project.

2	Face board	3/4" X 2-1/4" X 88-1/2"
2	Trim	3/4" X 1-3/4" X 88-1/2"
1	Face board	3/4" X 4-5/8" X 21-1/4"
1	Face board	3/4" X 3-3/4" X 21-1/4"
1	Face board	3/4" X 2-1/4" X 21-1/4"
1	Lower face board	3/4" X 1" X 21-1/4"
6	Shelves (plywood)	3/4" X 19-3/4" X 29-5/8"
1	Top (plywood)	3/4" X 19-3/4" X 29-5/8"
2	Corner strip	1-1/2" X 1-1/2" X 88-1/2"
1	Fascia trim	1/2" X 3/4" X 23-5/8"
1	Fascia trim	1/2" X 1" X 23-5/8"
1	Crown base	3/4" X 4-1/2" X 26-1/2"
2	Crown base	3/4" X 2" X 4-1/2"
1	Crown molding	11/16" X 1-3/4" X 26-1/2"
2	Crown molding	11/16" X 1-3/4" X 2"
2	Glass stiles	3/4" X 2-1/4" X 39-1/4"
2	Glass rails	3/4" X 2-1/4" X 16-5/8"
1	Mullion	1/2" X 3/4" X 35-1/4"
2	Muntins	1/2" X 3/4" X 17-1/8"
2	Strips	1/4" X 1/2" X 35-1/4"
2	Strips	1/4" X 1/2" X 16-5/8"
2	Door stiles	3/4" X 2-1/4" X 28-1/4"
2	Door rails	3/4" X 2-1/4" X 16-5/8"
1	Panel (hardboard)	1/4" X 17-3/8" X 24-1/2"
2	Back panels	3/4" X 19-3/8" X 88-1/2"
1	Glass pane	17" X 35-1/4"

Construction Procedure

1. Cut the two 88-1/2" face boards and trim pieces to the dimensions given in the cut list, and rip each joining edge of each set to a 22-1/2-degree angle. Cut the two 88-1/2" corner strips, then cut the two back panels to size. Miter-cut the back pieces' joining edges.

2. Fasten the trim pieces and back panels to the corner strips with glue and 1-1/2" finish nails. The back panels will have to be toenailed into the strips and set flush.

3. Cut the six shelves and top to the sizes indicated. Use a coping saw to cut 1-1/2" X 1-1/2" notches in the front corners of each piece to accommodate the corner strips.

4. Fasten the bottom shelf and the top with glue and 1-1/2" finish nails driven from the back and through the trim. Then, measuring from the bottom, fasten the remaining shelves at these locations: 14-1/2", 32", 44-3/4", 58-1/2", and 70".

5. Fit the remaining vertical face boards against the trim pieces and secure them to the shelves with glue and 1-1/2" finish nails. Fasten all the horizontal face boards in the same manner. Set all nail heads below the surface.

6. Cut the two facia trim pieces and fasten them to the center face boards with glue and 1" nails set below the surface.

7. Cut the crown base and molding to fit the cabinet, using the dimensions given as a guide. The ends of all pieces should be mitered to a 22-1/2-degree angle. Fasten the base first, then the molding, to the upper face board with 1" brads set below the surface.

8. Cut the door rails and stiles to the dimensions indicated. Use the table saw to cut a 1/4" X 3/8" rabbet into the inside edges of the back faces. Use a marking gauge or doweling jig to locate one dowel point at each corner joint. Drill 3/8" holes 3/4"-deep into the rails and stiles at the marked locations. Glue and dowel the door frame together with 3/8" X 1-1/8" dowels and clamp. Cut the hardboard panel to size and fasten it from the back side with 3/4" brads driven into the edges of the frame.

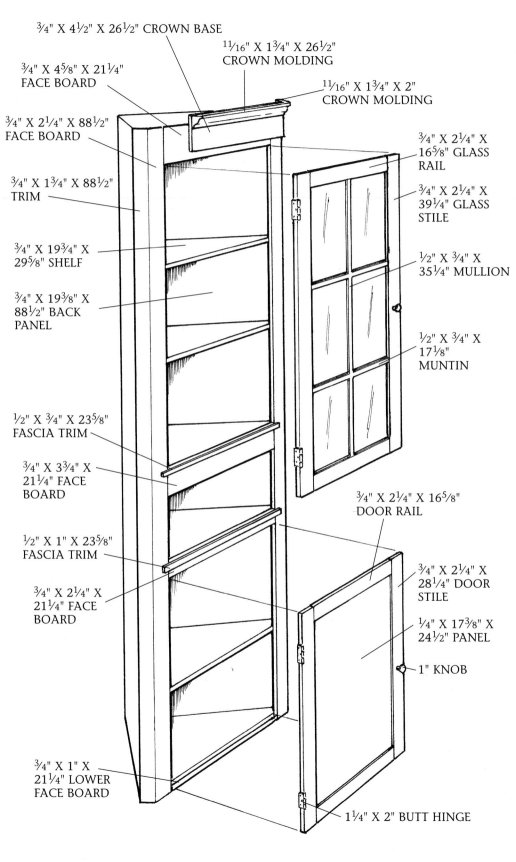

¾" X 4½" X 26½" CROWN BASE

¹¹⁄₁₆" X 1¾" X 26½"
CROWN MOLDING

¹¹⁄₁₆" X 1¾" X 2"
CROWN MOLDING

¾" X 4⅝" X 21¼"
FACE BOARD

¾" X 2¼" X 88½"
FACE BOARD

¾" X 1¾" X 88½"
TRIM

¾" X 19¾" X
29⅝" SHELF

¾" X 19⅜" X
88½" BACK
PANEL

½" X ¾" X 23⅝"
FASCIA TRIM

¾" X 3¾" X
21¼" FACE
BOARD

½" X 1" X 23⅝"
FASCIA TRIM

¾" X 2¼" X
21¼" FACE
BOARD

¾" X 1" X
21¼" LOWER
FACE BOARD

¾" X 2¼" X
16⅝" GLASS
RAIL

¾" X 2¼" X
39¼" GLASS
STILE

½" X ¾" X
35¼" MULLION

½" X ¾" X
17⅛"
MUNTIN

¾" X 2¼" X 16⅝"
DOOR RAIL

¾" X 2¼" X
28¼" DOOR
STILE

¼" X 17⅜" X
24½" PANEL

1" KNOB

1¼" X 2" BUTT HINGE

9. Repeat the procedure with the glass rails and stiles, but cut the rabbets 1/16" deeper. Do not install the glass after the joints have dried, but fit the frame to the cabinet's upper opening and mark the position of the shelves on the frame stiles. Use a chisel to cut 1/2" X 3/4" notches into the stiles at the marked points, and into the rails at the center.

10. Trim the glass mullion and the muntins to fit the frame notches. Then half-lap each muntin to mullion joint by making cuts of approximately 3/8" in depth in each piece. Glue the completed grille to the glass frame. Turn the frame over and set the glass in place. Then cut the stop strips to fit the frame rabbets and secure them with 1" brads driven from the sides.

11. Position and hang the glass and door frames using 1-1/4" X 2" butt hinges placed 2-1/2" from each corner, using the hardware provided. Fasten the magnetic catches to the unhinged stiles and the cabinet.

12. Sand the project and finish it as desired. Install 1" knobs to the midpoint of the door and glass stiles.

dish service

Perfect for an out of the way corner, and open and inviting besides. The service extends about a foot from the wall, with a 2-foot width. Its 40" overall height allows room for two dish sets and a few other things you might want to add.

Suggested Tools

Table saw

Jigsaw

Backsaw

3/8" Drill

1/16" Drill bit

1/8" Drill bit

No. 6 screw bit

3/8" Forstner bit

Hammer

Try Square

Marking Gauge

Tape Measure

Hardware and Supplies

Flush shelf hangers

No. 6 X 1-1/2" cabinet screws

10-Gauge X 1" cup hooks

18-Gauge X 3/4" brads

Aliphatic resin glue

Wood filler

Semi-gloss enamel paint

Cut List

White pine and A-C interior plywood are recommended for this project.

2	Back posts	3/4" X 1-1/2" X 40"
2	Upper posts	3/4" X 1-1/2" X 16"
2	Mid posts	3/4" X 1-1/2" X 6-1/2"
2	Lower posts	3/4" X 1-1/2" X 10-5/8"
2	Front rails	3/4" X 1-1/2" X 22-1/4"
2	Back rails	3/4" X 1-1/2" X 22-1/4"
2	Side rails	3/4" X 1-1/2" X 7"
2	Side rails	3/4" X 1-1/2" X 5-1/2"
2	Side brackets	3/4" X 5-1/4" X 5-1/2"
1	Rear bracket	3/4" X 6-3/4" X 22-1/4"
1	Top shelf (plywood)	3/4" X 11-1/2" X 23-3/4"
1	Mid shelf (plywood)	3/4" X 10-3/8" X 23-3/4"
1	Back (hardboard)	1/4" X 23-5/8" X 29-1/2"
2	Trim molding	3/4" X 11-3/4"
2	Trim molding	3/4" X 10-5/8"
2	Trim molding	3/4" X 24-1/8"
10	Dowel	3/8" X 12"
8	Dowel	3/8" X 9-7/8"
2	Dowel	3/8" X 9-1/4"
2	Dowel	3/8" X 7-3/4"
2	Dowel	3/8" X 23"
10	Dowel	3/8" X 1"

Construction Procedure

1. Cut all the 3/4" X 1-1/2" posts and rails to the sizes indicated in the cut list. Trim the 3/8" dowel rods into the lengths shown as well.

2. Use the table saw to cut a 1/4" X 3/8" rabbet into one edge of each back post. Then mark points at 2-1/2", 14-1/2", 21", and 30-7/8" from each post's top end along the front edge.

3. Locate and drill 3/8" X 1/2"-deep dowel holes 3/4" below the 14-1/2" and the 30-7/8" marks, and 3/4" above the 2-1/2" and 21" marks on the edge of both posts. Position the top edges of the 7" and 5-1/2" side rails at the marks and mark for matching holes in the ends of those pieces. Likewise, mark dowel holes at their opposite ends, then at the front and rear edges of the two mid

posts, and at the rear edges of the lower posts. Drill 3/8" dowel holes 1/2" deep.

4. Cut 3/4" X 1-1/2" notches into the four corners of the top shelf and the rear corners of the mid shelf.

5. Locate dowel holes for the upper rack along the top edge of the front and side rails. At the sides, the

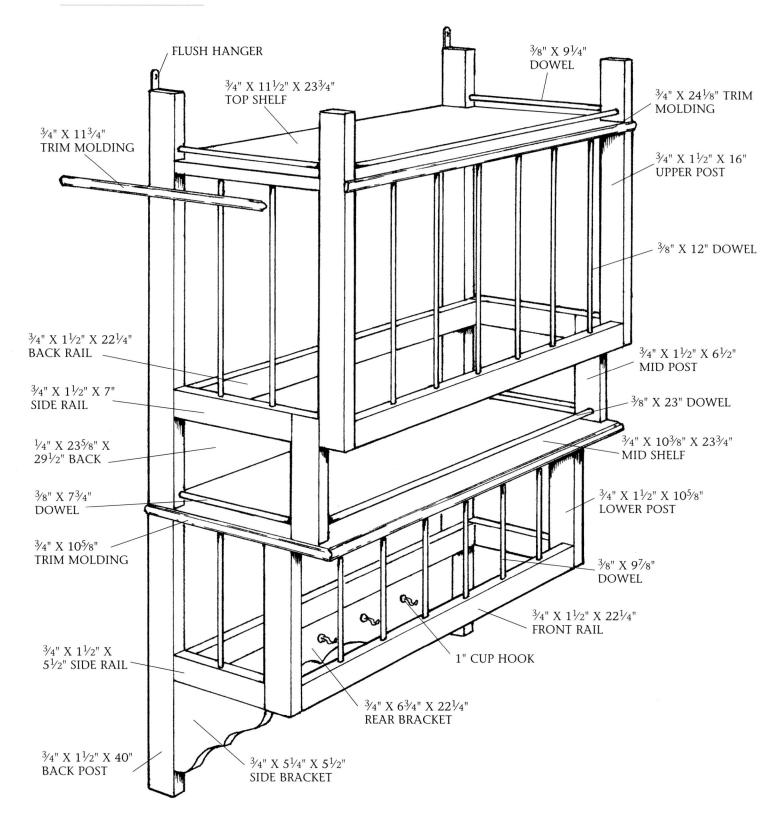

FLUSH HANGER

3/4" X 11 1/2" X 23 3/4"
TOP SHELF

3/8" X 9 1/4"
DOWEL

3/4" X 24 1/8" TRIM
MOLDING

3/4" X 11 3/4"
TRIM MOLDING

3/4" X 1 1/2" X 16"
UPPER POST

3/8" X 12" DOWEL

3/4" X 1 1/2" X 22 1/4"
BACK RAIL

3/4" X 1 1/2" X 6 1/2"
MID POST

3/4" X 1 1/2" X 7"
SIDE RAIL

3/8" X 23" DOWEL

1/4" X 23 5/8" X
29 1/2" BACK

3/4" X 10 3/8" X 23 3/4"
MID SHELF

3/8" X 7 3/4"
DOWEL

3/4" X 1 1/2" X 10 5/8"
LOWER POST

3/4" X 10 5/8"
TRIM MOLDING

3/8" X 9 7/8"
DOWEL

3/4" X 1 1/2" X 22 1/4"
FRONT RAIL

1" CUP HOOK

3/4" X 1 1/2" X
5 1/2" SIDE RAIL

3/4" X 6 3/4" X 22 1/4"
REAR BRACKET

3/4" X 1 1/2" X 40"
BACK POST

3/4" X 5 1/4" X 5 1/2"
SIDE BRACKET

two are 2-13/16" apart; at the front, the six are 3-3/16" apart. Transfer the hole placement to the top shelf by measuring from the corner notches. Drill all holes 3/8" X 1/2" deep.

6. Locate the dowels for the lower rack in the same manner. The spacing for the front rail is the same; for the side rail the single dowel is centered at 2-3/4" from either end. When transferring hole placement to the mid shelf, center the front rail with its back edge 7-3/4" from the shelf's rear edge to mark. Drill the dowel holes.

7. Cut the two side brackets and the rear bracket to the sizes indicated in the list. Cut a 1/4" X 3/8" rabbet into the upper edge of the rear bracket. Then mark a decorative profile, using the photo and illustration as a guide, along the lower edge of each piece in pencil. Cut to shape with a jigsaw.

8. Glue all the vertical dowels to their respective parts: The two front rails, and the four side rails. Set aside to dry.

9. Glue and dowel the two lower side rails to the back and lower posts. Lay flat and allow to dry.

10. Fasten the two side assemblies to the ends of the back and front rails as shown, using glue and No. 6

X 1-1/2" cabinet screws driven from the sides. Countersink the openings slightly to allow room for the filler. The back rail should be flush with the ends of the side rails, so a 5-1/2" gap exists between the front and back rails.

11. Fasten the rear and side brackets to the back posts using glue and No. 6 X 1-1/2" screws set into the wood at a 45-degree angle. Countersink the holes by 1/4". (The rear bracket's rabbet must face to the rear.) Fasten the front of the side brackets to the side rails in the same manner.

12. Apply glue to the tips of the lower set of dowels and the lower posts, and slip the mid shelf into position so the dowels are all in place and the shelf notches are firmly against the back posts. Fasten the shelf to the top ends of the lower posts using No. 6 X 1-1/2"screws.

13. Drill 3/8" X 1/2" dowel holes 3/4" above the lower ends of the mid posts, centered on the rear edge and sides. Glue and dowel the upper side rails to the back posts and the mid posts, with the side and front dowels in place. Fasten the mid posts' lower ends to the shelf with No. 6 X 1-1/2" screws.

14. Dry-fit the upper posts to the upper edges of the mid posts and

mark for the horizontal dowel holes. They should be located 3/4" from the top ends. Drill both the side and front dowel sockets 3/8" X 1/2" deep. Glue and dowel the mid posts at the bottom, and glue the three horizontal dowels in place at the top.

15. Slip the upper shelf in place at the level of the marked points on the back posts. Fasten it with two No. 6 X 1-1/2" screws angled into the posts from the rear, and with two screws countersunk into the side of the posts at the front.

16. Cut the 3/4" trim molding to the lengths indicated in the list and fit it in place around the two shelves by mitering the front corners. Fasten with 3/4" brads, predrilling the holes in the trim to keep it from splitting.

17. Glue the 1/4" X 23-5/8" X 29-1/2" hardboard panel to the rabbets in the rear of the frame and the back edge of the mid shelf. Fasten the panel with 3/4" brads along the top and sides, and at the mid shelf.

18. Finish the service with several coats of paint. When it's dry, attach the two flush shelf hangers to the rear of the back posts, and screw the five cup hooks into the rear bracket, 3" from the upper edge and spaced 3-3/4" apart.

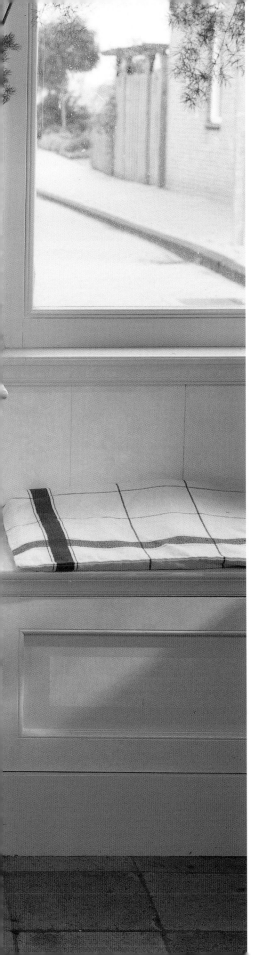

window bank

Nearly ten feet long but only 16" deep, this bank of window seats offers a sunny place to relax, but also provides storage space for all sorts of things in the cabinet shelves beneath. Some construction lumber is used in framing, but the cases are basically held together through the use of 3/4" plywood or medium-density fiberboard. The broad base plinths serve as decoration and lower shelf supports.

Suggested Tools

Table saw
Circular saw
Jigsaw
3/8" Drill
No. 6 screw bit
No. 8 screw bit
1/8" Drill bit
Router
3/8" Roundover bit
1/2" Chisel
Level
Tape measure
Hammer
Nail set

Hardware and Supplies

No. 6 X 1-1/4" cabinet screws
No. 8 X 1-1/4" cabinet screws
No. 8 X 1-1/2" cabinet screws
No. 8 X 3" wood screws
16-Gauge X 1-1/2" finish nails
18-Gauge X 1" brads
1-1/4" X 1-3/4" Butt hinges
Magnetic catches
Knob hardware
Wood filler
Aliphatic resin glue
Latex paint

Cut List

Medium-density fiberboard or A-C interior plywood, and Southern pine or Douglas fir, are recommended for this project.

1	Case rail	3/4" X 1-1/2" X 27-1/2"
1	Mid rail	3/4" X 1-1/2" X 24-1/2"
1	Base rail	3/4" X 1-1/2" X 24-1/2"
2	Case sides	3/4" X 1-1/2" X 25-1/4"
1	Front rail	1" X 1-3/4" X 27-1/2"
1	Cove molding	11/16" X 1-1/2" X 32"
2	Cove molding	11/16" X 1-1/2" X 16"
2	Cabinet sides (MDF)	3/4" X 14-1/4" X 26-3/4"
1	Top (MDF)	3/4" X 15-1/4" X 30-1/2"
2	Shelves (MDF)	3/4" X 12-1/2" X 27-1/2"
1	Shelf spacer (MDF)	3/4" X 2" X 27-1/2"
1	Plinth (MDF)	1" X 4-3/4" X 31"
2	Plinth returns (MDF)	1" X 4-3/4" X 3-1/2"
4	Seat rails	1-1/2" X 1-3/4" X 41"
4	Seat stretchers	1-1/2" X 1-3/4" X 11-3/4"
2	Shelf supports	3/4" X 1-1/2" X 41"
2	Shelf spacers	3/4" X 2" X 41"
2	Seat plinths (MDF)	1" X 4-3/4" X 43-1/2"
2	End plinths (MDF)	1" X 4-3/4" X 12-3/4"
2	Seat shelves (MDF)	3/4" X 11" X 41"
2	Seats (MDF)	3/4" X 12-3/4" X 43-1/2"
2	Cove molding	11/16" X 1-1/2" X 43"
2	Cove molding	11/16" X 1-1/2" X 12-1/2"
2	Seat ends (MDF	3/4" X 11-3/4" X 17"
4	Door panels	3/4" X 10-1/2" X 20-1/4"
12	Seat panel stiles	3/4" X 2" X 10-1/2"
12	Seat panel rails	3/4" X 2" X 16-1/4"
1	Cabinet door panel	3/4" X 21-3/4" X 27-1/4"
2	Door panel stiles	3/4" X 2" X 21-3/4"
2	Door panel rails	3/4" X 2" X 23-1/4"
12	Profile molding	1/2" X 3/4" X 6-1/2"
12	Profile molding	1/2" X 3/4" X 16-1/4"
2	Profile molding	1/2" X 3/4" X 17-3/4"
2	Profile molding	1/2" X 3/4" X 23-1/4"

$^{11}/_{16}$" X 1$^{1}/_{2}$" X 32" COVE MOLDING

$^{3}/_{4}$" X 1$^{1}/_{2}$" X 25$^{1}/_{4}$" CASE SIDE

1" X 1$^{3}/_{4}$" X 27$^{1}/_{2}$" FRONT RAIL

$^{3}/_{4}$" X 10$^{1}/_{2}$" X 20$^{1}/_{4}$" DOOR PANEL

$^{3}/_{4}$" X 2" X 10$^{1}/_{2}$" SEAT PANEL STILE

$^{3}/_{4}$" X 2" X 16$^{1}/_{4}$" SEAT PANEL RAIL

$^{1}/_{2}$" X $^{3}/_{4}$" X 17$^{3}/_{4}$" PROFILE MOLDING

$^{3}/_{4}$" X 2" X 27$^{1}/_{2}$" SHELF SPACER

1" X 4$^{3}/_{4}$" X 31" PLINTH

$^{3}/_{4}$" X 21$^{3}/_{4}$" X 27$^{1}/_{4}$" CABINET DOOR PANEL

$^{3}/_{4}$" X 2" X 23$^{1}/_{4}$" DOOR PANEL RAILS

$^{3}/_{4}$" X 2" X 21$^{3}/_{4}$" DOOR PANEL STILES

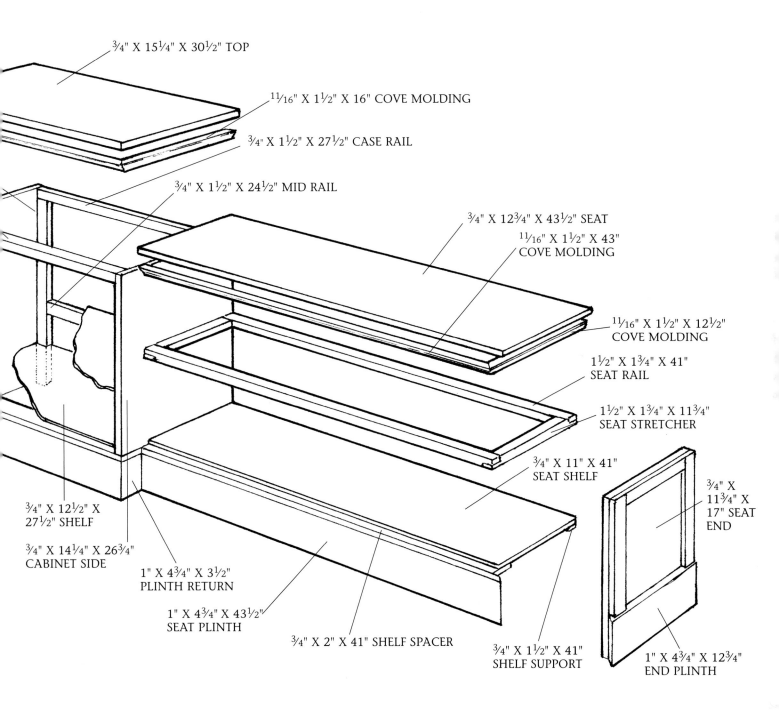

¾" X 15¼" X 30½" TOP

¹¹⁄₁₆" X 1½" X 16" COVE MOLDING

¾" X 1½" X 27½" CASE RAIL

¾" X 1½" X 24½" MID RAIL

¾" X 12¾" X 43½" SEAT

¹¹⁄₁₆" X 1½" X 43"
COVE MOLDING

¹¹⁄₁₆" X 1½" X 12½"
COVE MOLDING

1½" X 1¾" X 41"
SEAT RAIL

1½" X 1¾" X 11¾"
SEAT STRETCHER

¾" X 11" X 41"
SEAT SHELF

¾" X
11¾" X
17" SEAT
END

¾" X 12½" X
27½" SHELF

¾" X 14¼" X 26¾"
CABINET SIDE

1" X 4¾" X 3½"
PLINTH RETURN

1" X 4¾" X 43½"
SEAT PLINTH

¾" X 2" X 41" SHELF SPACER

¾" X 1½" X 41"
SHELF SUPPORT

1" X 4¾" X 12¾"
END PLINTH

Construction Procedure

1. The cabinets can be assembled as separate units, and the seat bank scaled for length as needed. Start construction with the main cabinet, by cutting the case rails and sides to length. Locate a place on the wall with accessible framing members and fasten the back rail and side pieces to it using No. 8 X 3" wood screws. The rail should be level, and butted to the upper ends of the plumbed side pieces. Then fasten the mid rail to the wall with its upper edge at a point 15-1/2" above floor level, and the base rail in the same manner, 4" above floor level.

2. Cut the cabinet sides and the two shelves to the sizes indicated. Fasten the sides to the framing just installed on the wall with six No. 6 X 1-1/4" cabinet screws along each edge, spaced 5" apart. Attach the front rail from the corners using No. 8 X 1-1/4" cabinet screws.

3. Use a jigsaw to cut 3/4" X 1-1/2" notches into the rear corners of each shelf piece. Set the shelves on top of the mid and base rails, level them, and secure them using No. 8 X 1-1/2" screws driven from the cabinet sides.

4. Cut the plinth from 1" MDF and miter the ends to 45 degrees. Cut the shelf spacer and place it with its upper edge against the bottom of the

lower shelf, front edges flush with the sides. Then fasten it through the cabinet sides using two No. 8 X 1-1/2" 3 cabinet screws at each joint. Nail the plinth to the front edges of the cabinet at the base using 16-gauge X 1-1/2" finish nails. Set the heads.

5. Cut the top to size. Use a roundover bit in the router to radius both the upper and lower edges of the two sides and front. Fasten the top to the case rails using No. X 1-1/2" screws counterbored through the bottom of the rail members and into the lower face of the top piece. Set the bit stop to 2" to avoid penetrating the top's surface.

6. Miter-cut and fit the cove molding against the front and sides, and beneath the top. Nail it in place with 16-gauge X 1-1/2" finish nails.

7. Cut the cabinet door panel to the size indicated, but measure the cabinet opening first to make any necessary adjustments. Then cut the false rails and stiles and fasten them to the surface of the door panel, rails butted against stile ends, with No. 6 X 1-1/4" cabinet screws countersunk and fastened from the back.

8. Miter-cut the profile molding to the sizes indicated and fasten it to the inner edges of the rails and stiles with 18-gauge X 1" brads. Set the

heads. Install two butt hinges at the edge of the door, 2" from the upper and lower edges, using the hardware provided. Fasten a magnetic catch and place the knob 8" below the upper edge.

9. Measure for the length of each seat bank. The entire unit can be fit between two walls or the ends can be closed and finished. Begin construction by cutting the seat rails and stretchers to length. (If you plan to finish the ends, remember that the end panel and false trim will finish out at 1-1/2" in thickness.) Then half-lap the corner joints so the rail tongues will rest upon those of the stretchers. (See page 48.)

10. Cut the shelf supports to the same length as the rails. Fasten the shelf supports and the rear rails to the wall so their upper edges are 4" and 17, respectively, from the floor. Assemble the stretchers to the front rails initially by fastening the corners using No. 6 X 1-1/4 countersunk screws. Cut the seat ends if needed.

11. Fit the assemblies into the mounted rails, level the stretchers, and fasten the seat ends to the frames using No. 6 X 1-1/4" cabinet screws spaced 4-1/4" apart. Fasten the inner stretchers to the face of the cabinet using three No. 8 X 1-1/2" screws spaced 5-1/2" apart.

12. Miter-cut the end plinths and fasten them to the bottom of the panels using 16-gauge X 1-1/2" finish nails. Place the seat plinths in position and mark the points at which they meet the inside edges of the seat ends. Cut a 1/2" X 3/4" rabbet into the inside edge of each plinth from that point all the way to the end which meets the cabinet. Clean the stopped end of the rabbet with a chisel. Cut a reverse miter into the cabinet end of each plinth.

13. Attach the plinths to the edge of the seat ends with finish nails, and cut and install the plinth returns to the cabinet using finish nails. Toe-nail each seat plinth and return together from the inside.

14. Cut and fit the shelf spacers against the rabbets in the seat plinths. Fasten the spacers from the ends using countersunk No. 8 X 1-1/2" cabinet screws.

15. Place the shelves on top of the rear supports and front spacer and fasten them from the ends using No. 8 X 1-1/2" cabinet screws.

16. Cut the false rails and stiles for the seat ends and fasten them to the panels using the same method as used on the door panel before. Cut, fit, and nail the profile moldings.

17. Cut the seats using the actual dimensions as a guide. Rout the top and bottom edges with a roundover bit. Install them from the bottom as before, then cut and nail in place the cove moldings at the front and sides.

18. Cut the four door panels, using the openings as a guide. Cut and fit the rails and stiles onto each door panel using the method described earlier. Cut and fit the profile moldings and fasten them with 1" brads.

19. Install the butt hinge sets onto each finished door using the hardware provided. On these smaller doors, the hinges should be positioned 3/4" from the upper and lower edges. Fasten the magnetiuc catches and knob assemblies.

20. Fill all exposed screw and nail holes with wood filler and paint the cabinet as desired. If you want to use the two-tone motif as in the photo, you can either mask the first-painted surfaces or trial-fit the components before painting and final assembly.

bookshelf couch & table

Here are two easy-to-build, space-saving projects that work well in a play-room or casual room. The three-piece suite in the photo is built to fit a bi-level floor, but it can be made for a flat surface as well. The tabletop lifts for storage; the bookshelf couch can be made separately if desired.

Cut List

Pine or spruce, or cabinet-grade plywood, is recommended for this project. Tongue-and-groove boards should be used for the backrests and table top if possible.

COUCH

6	Center and Sides	3/4" X 7-1/4" X 30"
4	Front and Back	3/4" X 7-1/4" X 47-1/4"
3	Backrest boards (T & G)	3/4" X 7-1/4" X 45-3/4"
1	Backrest board (T & G)	3/4" X 2-3/4" X 45-3/4"
3	Back stanchions	3/4" X 6-1/2" X 23-3/4"
1	Base board	3/4" X 6-1/2" X 45-3/4"
1	Cap board	3/4" X 2-3/8" X 45-3/4"
2	Rear supports	3/4" X 2" X 10"
4	Front supports	3/4" X 2" X 6"
2	Dowel	3/4" X 45-3/4"
6	Corner braces	3/4" X 1-1/2" X 8-1/2"
1	Canvas	23-3/4" X 60"
4	Cushions	4" X 23-1/2" X 23-1/2"

BOOKCASE

2	Sides	3/4" X 6-1/2" X 33"
2	Dividers	3/4" X 6-1/2" X 32-1/4"
1	Base	3/4" X 6-1/2" X 76-1/2"
1	Shelf	3/4" X 11-1/4" X 24-3/4"
1	Cap	3/4" X 8-7/8" X 78"
1	Fascia	3/4" X 3-1/2" X 78"
4	Trim	3/4" X 3/4" X 29"
1	Baseboard	3/4" 1-1/4" X 80-1/4"

CORNER TABLE

8	Side boards	3/4" X 7-1/4" X 30-3/4"
4	Top boards (T & G)	3/4" X 7-1/4" X 31-1/2"
1	Top board (T & G)	3/4" X 2-1/2" X 31-1/2"
4	Corner braces	3/4" X 1-1/2" X 14"
3	Batten boards	3/4" X 1-1/2" X 30"

Suggested Tools

Table saw

Circular saw

Jigsaw

3/8" Drill

No. 8 screw bit

3/4" Spade bit

Phillips-head driver bit

Straightedge

Try square

Tape measure

Palm sander

Hammer

Nail set

Hardware and Supplies

No. 8 X 1-1/4" wood screws

6-Penny Finish nails

Aliphatic resin glue

Wood filler

Polyurethane

Construction Procedure

1. Cut the center and side pieces to length. On one of the boards, measure 2-1/2" down from one edge and 8" in from one end and bore a 3/4" hole at that point. At the opposite end, mark a point 2-1/2" down from the edge, then rip a 2-1/2" strip, straight through the hole, from the board. Beginning at the hole and ending at a point 2" from the opposite end, with a jigsaw cut a 2-1/2"-deep curved relief in the board as shown.

2. Cut the six corner braces and fasten them vertically to the lower side boards so they're flush with the ends, using glue and No. 8 X 1-1/4" wood screws, countersunk to the surface. Similarly, place the braces on opposite sides of the lower center piece and fasten. The upper ends should extend beyond the boards.

3. Cut the two rear supports from 4" X 10" stock. Drill a 3/4" hole in each blank before cutting, then split the blank. Cut the front supports from two 2" X 12" pieces. Drill 3/4"

holes in the center of each, then halve each at the midpoint. Fasten the rear set horizontally so each one's upper edge is 2-1/2" from the edge of the upper side board—hole to the front—and the front set vertically, flush with the front edge of the side board. The remaining two supports should be fastened at the front edge of the drilled center piece so their top ends are 7-1/4" from the lower edge of the board. All supports should be glued and secured with four No. 8 X 1-1/4" screws.

4. Cut the front and back boards. Cut a 4" X 44" notch in the top of one back board. Fasten the lower pieces to the ends of the lower side boards using glue and No. 8 X 1-1/4" screws driven from the face and spaced 5-1/4" apart. The screws can be sunk and the holes filled, or you can use brass screws, set them flush with the surface, and leave them exposed. Fasten the upper pieces to the ends of the upper side boards in the same manner, notched board at the back, but space the screws at the rear only 3" apart. Locate the screws in the middle to catch the front corner brace and supports, and the rear corner brace.

5. Cut the three back stanchions at a taper so the upper ends are 1-5/8" wide and the lower ones 6-1/2" in width. Cut the backrest boards, and the base board. Using countersunk

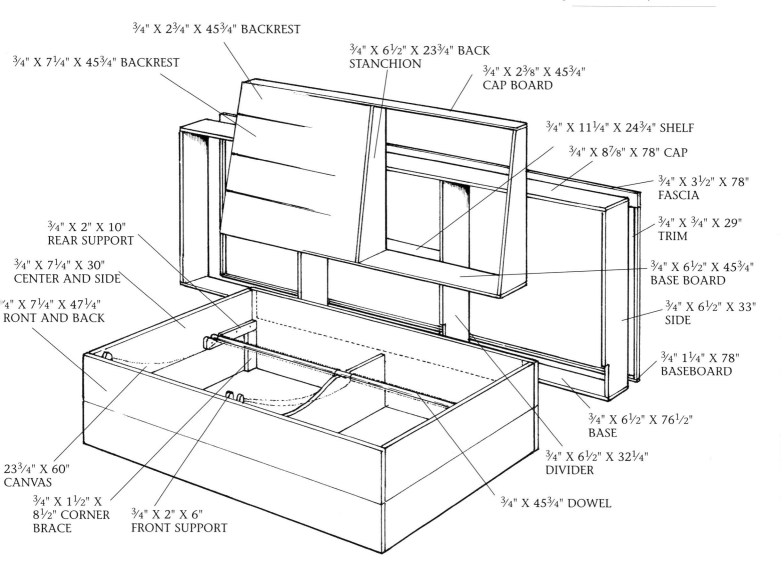

¾" X 2¾" X 45¾" BACKREST

¾" X 7¼" X 45¾" BACKREST

¾" X 6½" X 23¾" BACK STANCHION

¾" X 2⅜" X 45¾" CAP BOARD

¾" X 11¼" X 24¾" SHELF

¾" X 8⅞" X 78" CAP

¾" X 3½" X 78" FASCIA

¾" X ¾" X 29" TRIM

¾" X 6½" X 45¾" BASE BOARD

¾" X 6½" X 33" SIDE

¾" 1¼" X 78" BASEBOARD

¾" X 6½" X 76½" BASE

¾" X 6½" X 32¼" DIVIDER

¾" X 45¾" DOWEL

¾" X 2" X 10" REAR SUPPORT

¾" X 7¼" X 30" CENTER AND SIDE

¾" X 7¼" X 47¼" FRONT AND BACK

23¾" X 60" CANVAS

¾" X 1½" X 8½" CORNER BRACE

¾" X 2" X 6" FRONT SUPPORT

No. 8 X 1- 1/4" screws, fasten the four backrest boards to the tapered edges of the three stanchions, starting at the top with the narrowest board. The board should be flush at the top and with the end stanchions. The middle stanchion is centered.

6. Attach the base board to the lower ends of the stanchions using 1-1/4" screws. Do not cut or fasten the cap board yet, unless you don't plan to add the bookshelf.

7. Use three No. 8 X 1-1/4" screws per joint to fasten the back rest assembly to the edges of the center and rear supports. Cut the dowel to 45-3/4" in length. Cut the canvas in half and sew 1" borders at the sides. Sew the ends of the canvas slings into sleeves to fit the dowel.

8. The bookcase can be made to extend beyond the end of the couch to meet the end of the corner table. The backrest will have to be extended as well. Cut the base, cap board, two sides, and dividers to size.

9. Measure in 25-1/2" from each end of the base piece and mark. Cut a 3/4" X 14-1/2" notch in the front edge of the base where it will meet

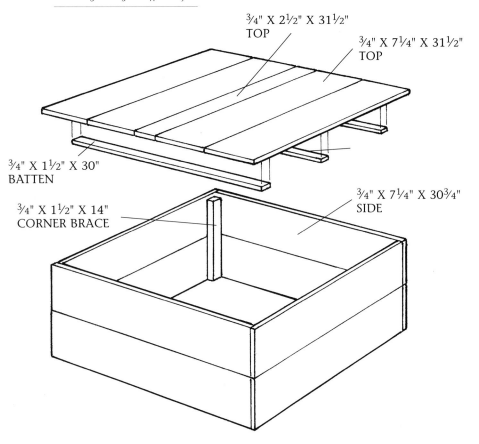

¾" X 2½" X 31½"
TOP

¾" X 7¼" X 31½"
TOP

¾" X 1½" X 30"
BATTEN

¾" X 1½" X 14"
CORNER BRACE

¾" X 7¼" X 30¾"
SIDE

the couch. Center a divider over each of the marks and fasten from the bottom with glue and two No. 8 X 1-1/4" screws. Cut a 3/4" X 14-1/2" notch in the lower front edge of the side and divider, then fasten the sides to the ends of the base piece in the same manner. Position the assembly against the rear of the couch frame and measure exactly the width and length of the cap piece. Cut and fasten it to the upper ends of the sides and dividers using glue and 1-1/4" countersunk screws.

10. Cut the shelf to length by measuring the distance between the dividers. Round the sharp front edges

of the board with a sander and fasten the shelf from the sides at midlevel using 1-1/4" screws.

11. Cut and fasten the baseboard strip to the edge of the base using 6-penny finish nails set beneath the surface. Cut the fascia board and install it in the same manner. Then measure and cut the four trim strips and nail them to the face edges of the sides and dividers, predrilling the nail holes to prevent splitting.

12. The corner table is assembled in the same way as the couch. Cut the side boards and the corner braces, then fasten the braces to the

boards in sets by butting the edges and aligning the ends of each set, and positioning the braces so one is flush to the ends and one is 3/4" from the opposite end. When connecting the four sides, the end of one is butted against the inside of the one before it. Use two screws per board when fastening the joints.

13. The five top boards are held together from the underside with three battens. Cut the battens to length then lay the top boards on a flat surface with the narrowest in the center. Align the ends and fasten the battens so they are centered, and spaced so the outer ones are 7/8" from the edge of the boards. Use glue and No. 8 X 1-1/4" screws to complete the joints.

14. Sand the corners and edges of all the components to give them a rounded appearance. Sand the surfaces of the wood and coat it with two layers of polyurethane. Sealer and paint can be used as a finish if desired.

15. Place the slings in position in the front and rear supports of each couch. You can purchase cushions to fit the seats and backs. If you need to fasten the lower part of the bookcase to the couch, you can do that from the outside by using a piece of quarter-round trim or baseboard nailed along the bottom edge of both pieces.

cd cabinet

Here's a neat and tidy case for storing all those CDs you'd otherwise leave lying around in stacks—up to 400 of them. There's also room for tapes in the drawers below. This project can be made with board stock or with medium-density fiberboard or cabinet-grade plywood.

Suggested Tools

- Table saw
- Dado blade
- 3/8" Drill
- 1/8" Drill bit
- Biscuit joiner
- Phillips screwdriver
- Hammer
- Tape measure
- Straightedge
- Pipe clamps

Hardware and Supplies

- No. 0 biscuits
- 1" Knobs
- 16-Gauge X 1" brads
- Aliphatic resin glue
- Light stain
- Polyurethane

Construction Procedure

1. Cut the top, sides, and shelves to the dimensions indicated in the list. If you are building with stock lumber, you'll probably have to edge-join the wood to achieve the panel widths for these parts. Reinforce the joints by placing a biscuit every 12" or so.

2. Cut the 12 6-3/8" and the one 4-1/8" dividers to the dimensions indicated.

Cut List

Poplar, clear-grained pine, and medium-density fiberboard are recommended for this project.

5	Shelves	3/4" X 13-3/4" X 25-3/4"
12	Dividers	3/4" X 6-3/8" X 13-3/4"
1	Divider	3/4" X 4-1/8" X 13-3/4"
1	Base	3/4" X 3-1/8" X 25-3/4"
2	Sides	3/4" X 13-3/4" X 36-1/2"
1	Top	3/4" X 14-3/4" X 28"
16	Drawer faces	3/4" X 5-3/4" X 6-1/4"
2	Drawer faces	3/4" X 3-7/8" X 12-1/4"
32	Drawer sides	3/8" X 6-1/4" X 13-1/4"
16	Drawer backs	3/8" X 5-1/4" X 5-3/4"
16	Drawer bottoms	1/8" X 5-1/4" X 12-7/8"
4	Drawer sides	3/8" X 3-7/8" X 13-1/4"
2	Drawer backs	3/8" X 3-3/8" X 12-1/4"
2	Drawer bottoms	1/8" X 12-1/4" X 12-7/8"
1	Back (MDF or hardboard)	1/4" X 27-1/4" X 36-1/2"

3. Mark lines across both faces of each of the top three shelves and the top of the fourth shelf at 6-7/16", 12-7/8", and 19-5/16" from one end. Mark the bottom of the fourth, and the top of the fifth shelf at 12-7/8" from one end.

4. Along each of these lines, center two points 10" apart. Likewise, center and mark two points 10" apart on each long edge of all the dividers. Use the biscuit joiner to cut the slots to complete each joint. It will require a tool that allows you to make a flat cut on the shelf surfaces by either adjusting the fence to 0 degrees, or removing it.

5. Glue and insert the 46 biscuits and, starting at the bottom, join the 13 dividers to the five shelves.

6. Cut the base piece to the dimensions indicated. Mark the slot placement for the joints at the ends of the shelves (10" apart) one at each end of the base, and two at the base's upper edge, placed 12" apart.

7. Glue and insert the two biscuits into the edge of the base and install it to the bottom shelf. Then glue and inser the remaining 22 biscuits at the edges of the shelves and base and carefully position the

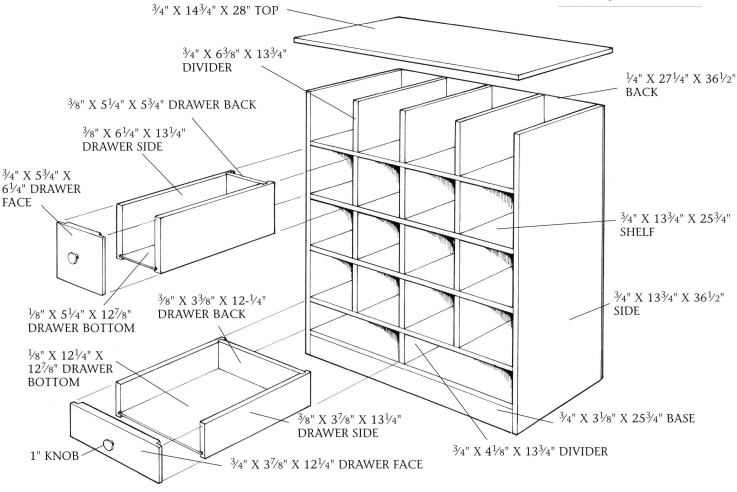

3/4" X 14 3/4" X 28" TOP

3/4" X 6 3/8" X 13 3/4" DIVIDER

3/8" X 5 1/4" X 5 3/4" DRAWER BACK

3/8" X 6 1/4" X 13 1/4" DRAWER SIDE

3/4" X 5 3/4" X 6 1/4" DRAWER FACE

1/8" X 5 1/4" X 12 7/8" DRAWER BOTTOM

3/8" X 3 3/8" X 12-1/4" DRAWER BACK

1/8" X 12 1/4" X 12 7/8" DRAWER BOTTOM

1" KNOB

3/4" X 3 7/8" X 12 1/4" DRAWER FACE

3/8" X 3 7/8" X 13 1/4" DRAWER SIDE

3/4" X 4 1/8" X 13 3/4" DIVIDER

1/4" X 27 1/4" X 36 1/2" BACK

3/4" X 13 3/4" X 25 3/4" SHELF

3/4" X 13 3/4" X 36 1/2" SIDE

3/4" X 3 1/8" X 25 3/4" BASE

sides to complete all the joints. Clamp the case together.

8. Center the top over the case with its back edge extending 1/4" over the sides' rear edges. Mark the position of the slots on the top for the remaining six divider biscuits and for the four side-to-top joints. Cut the top and the four remaining side slots, then glue and place the biscuits and position the top. Clamp.

9. Once the adhesive has dried, glue the back panel in place and tack

it to the case with 16-gauge X 1" brads placed 6" apart.

10. Cut all the drawer components to the sizes indicated, using the table saw. Install the dado blade in the saw and cut 3/8" X 3/8" rabbets into the back vertical edges of all the drawer faces. Then cut 3/8" X 1/8"-deep dadoes into the inside faces of all the drawer sides, 1/4" from the back ends.

11. Set your table-saw fence to cut a 1/8"-deep slot no more than 3/8" from the lower edge of each drawer

side, on the same face as the previous dado cuts.

12. Assemble each drawer unit by gluing the back into the side dadoes, with the bottoms installed in the slots. Then glue the faces to the front edges. Drill 1/8" holes through the center of each drawer face.

13. Sand the case lightly and stain it as desired. Finish with polyurethane or lacquer. Install the drawer knobs with 1-1/4" screws mounted from the back.

closet organizer

A room that needs something between a wardrobe and a walk-in closet could use this 15' modular add-on that isn't nearly as tough to tackle as a built-in remodeling job. It can be made as shown or constructed without the additional wardrobes at each end. Plywood or medium-density fiberboard are good material candidates.

Suggested Tools

Table saw	Tape measure
Circular saw	Framing square
Router	Combination square
3/8" Roundover bit	Straightedge
3/8" Drill	Level
1/8" Drill bit	Plumb bob
1/4" Drill bit	Chalk line
No. 6 screw bit	Hammer
No. 8 screw bit	Utility knife
Phillips-head driver bit	Sander

Cut List

Cabinet-grade plywood and commercial framing lumber are recommended for this project. Dimensions will vary with your rafter angles and site situation.

2	Nailers	1-1/2" X 3-1/2" X 48"
2	Nailers	1-1/2" X 3-1/2" X 66"
2	End panels	3/4" X 28" X 66"
2	Side panels	3/4" X 12" X 62"
4	Closet panels	3/4" X 28" X 86"
7	Divider panels	3/4" X 20" X 76"
2	Case sides	3/4" X 18-1/2" X 84"
1	Back (drywall)	5/8" X 16" X 56"
2	Backs (drywall)	5/8" X 49-1/2" X 56"
4	Wardrobe shelves	3/4" X 20" X 22-7/8"
2	Center shelves	3/4" X 14-1/2" X 18"
4	Center shelves	3/4" X 14-1/2" X 19-1/2"
4	Side shelves	3/4" X 15-1/4" X 19-1/2"
2	Side shelves	3/4" X 15-1/4" X 18"
2	Sliding shelves	3/4" X 13-1/2" X 18"
5	Drawer faces	3/4" X 8" X 14-1/4"
10	Drawer sides	1/2" X 6" X 18"
10	Drawer ends	1/2" X 6" X 12-1/2"
5	Drawer bottoms	1/4" X 13" X 17-1/2"
2	Header panels	3/4" X 5-1/2" X 30-1/2"
2	Header panels	3/4" X 5-1/2" X 48"
2	Track mounts	1" X 1" X 30-1/2"
2	Track mounts	1" X 1" X 48"
1	Fascia	3/4" X 11" X 14-1/2"
1	Light panel	3/4" X 9" X 14-1/2"
4	Base nailers	1-1/2" X 3-1/4" X 22-7/8"
4	Base nailers	1-1/2" X 3-1/4" X 14-1/2"
4	Base nailers	1-1/2" X 3-1/4" X 15-1/4"
2	Toe boards	3/4" X 3-1/4" X 22-7/8"
2	Toe boards	3/4" X 3-1/4" X 14-1/2"
2	Toe boards	3/4" X 3-1/4" X 15-1/4"
1	Tempered glass shelf	1/4" X 14-1/4" X 18"
1	Tempered glass shelf	1/4" X 14-1/4" X 15"
2	Tempered glass faces	1/4" X 4" X 14"

Hardware and Supplies

No. 6 X 3/4" cabinet screws
No. 6 X 1" cabinet screws
No. 6 X 1-5/8" drywall screws
No. 8 X 1-1/2" cabinet screws
No. 8 X 3-1/2" drywall screws
16-Gauge X 1-1/2" wire brads
6-Penny finish nails
16-Penny sinkers
Adjustable closet rod
1/4" Pin shelf supports
3/4" Corner braces
18" Bottom-mount drawer slides
18" Shelf slides
3-1/2" Drawer pulls
24" X 80" Bifold doors
48" Door track
30" X 60" Bifold panels
30" Door track
Aliphatic resin glue
Silicone sealant
Wood stain
Polyurethane

Construction Procedure

1. Measure the width, depth, and height of the space you intend to use. The width can be adjusted by shortening, lengthening, or eliminating the end units. If you're building against a pitched rafter ceiling, the angle of the rafters will dictate the length of the vertical members, since you will want to maintain the depth dimensions given in the cut list. Mark, in pencil, the planned location of all the vertical panels on your existing wall.

TOP VIEW

FRONT VIEW

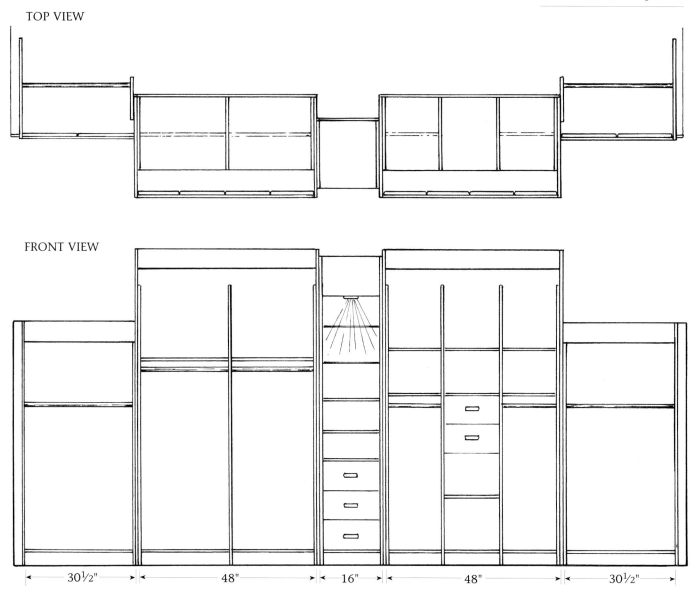

|← 30½" →| |←   48"   →| |← 16" →| |←   48"   →| |← 30½" →|

2. Assemble the center case first. Cut the two sides, the 18" bottom and center shelves, the toe board, and the fascia and light panel. (The exact height of the side pieces can be determined by checking against the floor-position measurements given in Step 5.) Use a 3/8" roundover bit in the router to round the front edges of the sides and the two shelves. Try the sides for fit in their place against the wall. (If your ceiling is uneven, you can cover the gaps at the top of the panels with quarter-round molding strips when the unit is complete.) Rather than build this case using furniture joinery, it will be easier to use external fasteners such as 3/4" corner, or chair, braces to hold the perpendicular parts together, and to secure the unit to the floor. The end panels are nailed to the walls before completion. In this assembly as with all others, each individual piece must be stained after the final cut is made, but prior to installation, as it would be difficult to achieve a consistent finish once the pieces were assembled.

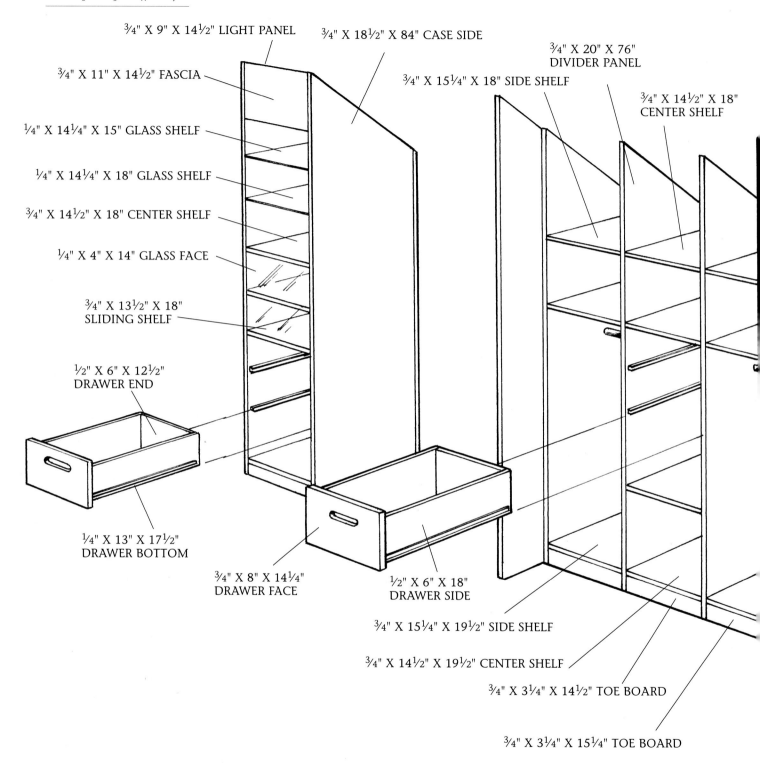

¾" X 9" X 14½" LIGHT PANEL

¾" X 18½" X 84" CASE SIDE

¾" X 20" X 76" DIVIDER PANEL

¾" X 15¼" X 18" SIDE SHELF

¾" X 14½" X 18" CENTER SHELF

¾" X 11" X 14½" FASCIA

¼" X 14¼" X 15" GLASS SHELF

¼" X 14¼" X 18" GLASS SHELF

¾" X 14½" X 18" CENTER SHELF

¼" X 4" X 14" GLASS FACE

¾" X 13½" X 18" SLIDING SHELF

½" X 6" X 12½" DRAWER END

¼" X 13" X 17½" DRAWER BOTTOM

¾" X 8" X 14¼" DRAWER FACE

½" X 6" X 18" DRAWER SIDE

¾" X 15¼" X 19½" SIDE SHELF

¾" X 14½" X 19½" CENTER SHELF

¾" X 3¼" X 14½" TOE BOARD

¾" X 3¼" X 15¼" TOE BOARD

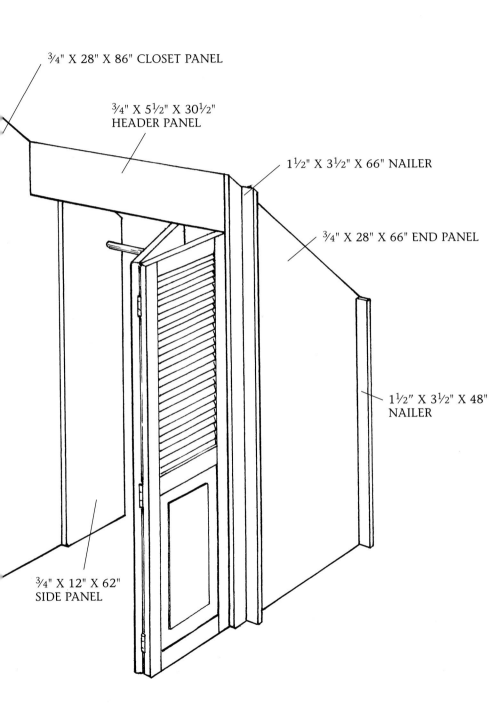

¾" X 28" X 86" CLOSET PANEL

¾" X 5½" X 30½"
HEADER PANEL

1½" X 3½" X 66" NAILER

¾" X 28" X 66" END PANEL

1½" X 3½" X 48"
NAILER

¾" X 12" X 62"
SIDE PANEL

From the bottom end of each side, measure 3-5/8", 4-11/16", 12-11/16, 20-11/16", 28-11/16", 36-11/16", 44-3/4", 54-3/4", and 64-3/4" on the inside faces and mark. These points indicate the centerlines of the shelves and the slides for mounting. Since slide designs can vary slightly, check before drilling to make sure there will be enough clearance between the drawer faces to allow them to close without binding. Mount the slides at the points that terminate with 11/16"; drill 1/2"-deep 1/4" shelf-support holes 14" and 11" apart at the 54-3/4" and 64-3/4" points; mount the fixed shelves with 3/4" screws and corner braces at the 3-5/8" and 44-3/4" points, rear edges flush. Recess the toe board with its face 3/4" from the front edge and fasten it to the sides and bottom shelf with braces. Then position the fascia and light panel at the top of the case and—after painting the boards—secure them with corner braces. If you plan on installing a light fixture, you'll need to drill the appropriate-sized hole in the light panel for the fixture beforehand.

3. Cut the front and rear nailers and end panels to fit against the walls. Paint the front edges of the front nailers to match the room decor. Space the nailers 1/2" less apart than the width of the panels and plumb them with a level before screwing or nailing them to the stud

framing you've located within the wall. Use No. 8 X 1-1/2" cabinet screws spaced about 18" apart to fasten the end panels in place.

4. Strike a chalk line on the floor between the forward edges of the two end panels. Measure forward 15-3/4" from this line and mark; this indicates the position for the front edge of the closet panels. Cut the four closet panels to fit the ceiling line, then use a 3/8" roundover bit in the router to round the front edges of each panel. Locate the outer panels at their marked places and secure them to the floor with corner braces, 18" back from the front edge on the

outside face and 5-1/2" from the edge on the inside face. Temporarily brace them to the ceiling in an inconspicuous location.

5. Prepare to put the center case into position with its front edges 12-3/4" forward of the chalk line. Cut two base nailers to 3-1/4" X 14-1/2" and screw them to the floor on edge so the case will form a perimeter around them (set the front nailer back a few inches so it won't interfere with the corner braces already in place.) Secure the case to the floor at the rear, inside, with corner braces and No. 8 screws. Check the case for square, then set 6-penny finish nails through the lower shelf and into the nailers below. Position the two remaining closet panels against the outside of the case, with their front edges 15-3/4" from the chalk line, and secure the panels to the side of the case using No. 8 X 1-1/2" cabinet screws spaced 18" apart in two vertical lines struck 5" from the panel's front edge and 8" from its rear. Drill and countersink the screw holes from the panel faces.

6. The seven divider panels are positioned with their front edges 7-3/4" forward of the chalk line. Cut them to the proper dimensions and rout the front edges to a 3/8" radius as before. Fasten each pair of end dividers to the closet panels already in place. The rear edges of all adjoin-

ing panels should be flush. Countersink the mounting holes from the inside, using the same schedule and screws as used on the last two closet panels.

7. Center the single divider panel between the left-hand set. Cut the four base nailers to 3-1/4" X 22-7/8" and screw them to the floor on edge, the front ones 1-1/2" from the dividers' front edges and the rear ones inset 1" from the rear edges. Then cut the two 22-7/8" toe boards and nail them against the front nailers with their faces 3/4" from the front edges of the dividers. Cut the four wardrobe shelves and radius their front edges. Then mount two with finish nails to the top of the nailers, with the rear edges flush to the rear of the dividers. The upper shelves are mounted 52" above the bottom set, using corner braces set 16" apart.

8. The remaining two dividers are assembled as a unit before they're placed within the right-hand set. On each one's inside face, mark from the bottom edge points at 3-5/8", 18-5/8", 30- 5/8", 38-5/8", 46-5/8", and 58-5/8". Cut the four remaining center shelves and round their front edges with the router and 3/8" roundover bit. Mount three of them, rear edges flush to the rear of the dividers, centered over the 18-5/8", 46-5/8", and 58-5/8" points, using corner braces and 3/4" screws. Fasten drawer slides at the 30-5/8" and 38-5/8" points. Cut two 3-1/4" X 14-1/2" base nailers and fasten each respectively on edge to the floor 1-1/2" from the dividers' front edges and 1" from their rear edges. Put the assembled unit into position and cut the last 14-1/2" toe board. Nail it to the front of the nailer. Set the bottom shelf into place and nail it to the nailers. Fasten the rear of the unit to the floor with 3/4" screws and braces.

9. Cut the four remaining 3-1/4" nailers to 15-1/4" in length and fasten them on edge in the same positions as the ones you just secured. Cut and nail the last two toe boards to fit over the nailers. Use corner braces on each divider between the nailers to hold the panels to the floor. Cut the six side shelves and rout their front edges to a 3/8" radius. Nail the bottom shelves in place, rear edges flush, then mount the middle and top shelves at the same level as the ones in the middle unit, using corner braces and 3/4" screws.

10. Cut the drywall sections to fit behind the two 48" closets and the center case. Fasten them to the back edges with No. 6 X 1-5/8" drywall screws. Cut the narrow side panels and fasten them to the outside faces of the closet panels so they extend 6-3/4" beyond the panels' back edges.

11. Cut the header panels and track mounts to fit their openings. Using No. 8 X 1-1/2" screws, fasten the mounting strips to the back of the headers so their lower edges are flush. Paint each assembly and allow to dry. Install the lower tracks for the bifold doors 3/4" behind the panels' front edges and measure the door heights. With each bifold unit, position the header panels to allow 1/4" to 3/8" clearance at the top and bottom, then fasten the headers to the side panels using corner braces and 3/4" screws. Use a plumb bob to help install the upper tracks directly above the lower ones. Paint and hang the bifold doors and panels.

12. Fasten the closet rods to the vertical panels at a point 2-3/4" below the wardrobe shelves. Secure them with 3/4" screws.

13. Cut the drawer sides and ends to the dimensions indicated. Cut a 1/4" X 1/4" dado 1/2" from the lower edge of each piece, then cut the drawer bottoms. Slip the bottoms into the dadoes and fasten the sides to the edges of the ends using glue and 1-1/2" wire brads set into the wood. Allow to dry. Mount the drawer slide brackets to the lower edges of the drawer units and slip them into place. Cut the drawer faces and use a roundover bit in the router to radius the edges slightly. Glue the faces to the mounted drawers and

adjust for clearance at the sides and between each face before securing them from the inside with No. 6 X 1" cabinet screws. Mark and install the drawer hardware.

14. Cut the two sliding shelves to size. Round the front edges with a 3/8" roundover bit, then cut a 3/8"-deep, 1/4"-wide slot into the upper face of each shelf 3/4" from the front edge. Mount the drawer slide brackets to the edges of the shelves, glue the edges of the tempered glass faces into the shelf slots with silicone sealant, and slip the shelves into place. Press the pin shelf supports into the 1/4" holes drilled to accept them, and mount the glass shelves.

bedfoot chest

Here's a different angle on the traditional foot-of-the-bed cedar chest—a set of bin-drawer cabinets that open from the front so you don't have to clear the top to get inside. The ones shown are made for a queen-size bed.

Suggested Tools

Table saw
Backsaw
Jigsaw
3/8" Drill
No. 8 screw bit
3/32" Drill bit
1/4" Drill bit
Combination square
Tape measure
Straightedge
Marking gauge
Dowel jig or centers (optional)
Hammer
Rasp
Pipe clamps
Sander

Hardware and Supplies

No. 8 X 1-1/4" wood screws
No. 8 X 2" wood screws
1-1/4" X 12" Piano hinge
1-1/4" X 25-1/2" Piano hinge
1/4" X 1-1/2" Dowel pegs
Aliphatic resin glue
Polyurethane or tung oil

Cut List

Red cedar or clear pine is recommended for this project.

SMALL UNIT

1	Top	3/4" X 13-3/4" X 15-3/4"
1	Bottom	3/4" X 12-1/4" X 14-1/4"
2	Sides	3/4" X 15" X 15-3/4"
1	Back	3/4" X 12-1/4" X 15"
1	Face	3/4" X 12-1/4" X 15"
1	Drawer bottom	3/4" X 12-1/4" X 14-1/4"
2	Drawer sides	3/4" X 13-1/4" X 13-1/4"
1	Stop	7/8" X 1" X 12-1/4"
4	Legs	1-3/4" X 1-3/4" X 4-1/4"

LARGE UNIT

1	Top	3/4" X 15-3/4" X 27-1/2"
1	Bottom	3/4" X 14-1/4" X 26"
2	Sides	3/4" X 15" X 15-3/4"
1	Back	3/4" X 15" X 26"
1	Face	3/4" X 15" X 26"
1	Drawer bottom	3/4" X 14-1/4" X 26"
2	Drawer sides	3/4" X 13-1/4" X 13-1/4"
1	Stop	7/8" X 1" X 26"
4	Legs	1-3/4" X 1-3/4" X 4-1/4"

Construction Procedure

1. Both cabinets are built using the same procedure. If you're not comfortable with the detail work involved in using dowel joints, you may substitute 2" finish nails driven from the face side and filled.

2. Cut the top, bottom, sides, and back to the dimensions given. On the back face of the top, measure in 3/8" from the back and side edges and strike a pencil line. Repeat on the lower and back edges of the sides, and on the lower edge of the

back. Mark and drill 1/2"-deep 1/4" holes along these lines as follows: on the top, starting 1" from the front, space them 4-1/2" apart at the sides, and starting 1-1/4" from the side, 3-3/4" apart along the back; on the sides, starting 2-1/4" from the front, space them 4" apart at the bottom, and starting 1" from the bottom, 4-1/4" apart at the back; and starting 1" from the side edge, 3-3/8" apart along the lower edge of the back. Using a dowel jig or insertable dowel centers, transfer the position of the

drilled holes to the edges of their mates, making sure that the joints at the rear are snug. Drill the 18 1/4" edge holes to a 1-1/8" depth.

3. Use glue and 1/4" X 1-1/2" dowel pegs to fasten the sides to the edges of the bottom and back pieces. Clamp until dry. Then glue, dowel, and clamp the top to the edges of the sides and back piece. Allow to dry.

4. Cut the four 1-3/4" X 1-3/4" legs to 4-1/4" in length. Mark a line

across all four faces of each one 1-3/4" from one end, which will be the top. Then, at the bottom, mark a line 1/2" to each side of a center point made on each face. Use a backsaw to cut from the 1-3/4" line to the 1" line at the bottom of each face, on all four legs. Position each leg so the square sides are flush with the joint edges of the bottom piece; the front legs should be flush to the forward edge as well. Fasten the legs from the top using glue and No. 8 X 2" countersunk wood screws spaced diagonally 1-1/2" apart.

5. Cut the face, drawer bottom, and two drawer side blanks to the dimensions given. The face and bottom may have to be trimmed on one side an extra 1/8" or so to allow clearance within the cabinet. Find a thin stick about 14" long and drill two holes through it, 13-1/4" apart. Place a nail in one hole and hold it in one corner of one of the sides, then put a pencil in the other hole and swing an arc across the face of the wood. Cut the arc with a jigsaw. Trace the outline onto the second side piece and cut an arc in it too.

6. Using a combination square, draw a pencil outline 3-1/2" wide by 3-3/4" tall in the center of the face panel, beginning 3" from the top edge. Recreate the heart as shown within this box, drill a 1/4" hole at the base of the heart, and carefully

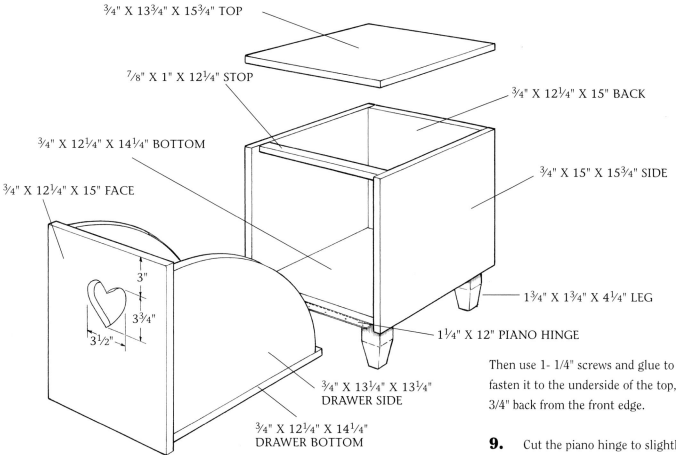

¾" X 13¾" X 15¾" TOP

⅞" X 1" X 12¼" STOP

¾" X 12¼" X 14¼" BOTTOM

¾" X 12¼" X 15" FACE

3"

3¾"

3½"

¾" X 13¼" X 13¼"
DRAWER SIDE

¾" X 12¼" X 14¼"
DRAWER BOTTOM

¾" X 12¼" X 15" BACK

¾" X 15" X 15¾" SIDE

1¾" X 1¾" X 4¼" LEG

1¼" X 12" PIANO HINGE

cut out the shape with a jigsaw. Use a rasp or file to smooth the edges.

7. On the back of the face and the surface of the bottom piece, measure 3/8" in from the sides, and 1-1/8" from the lower edge of the face. Mark a line across the boards at these points. On the face, measure in 1" from one side and mark points 3-3/8" apart along the lower line. Then measure 1-1/2" from the bottom and mark points 3-3/4" apart along both side lines. On the bottom piece, measure 1" from the forward edge and mark points 3-3/4" apart along both

lines. Drill 1/2"-deep 1/4" holes at these 15 points. Transfer the position of the drilled holes to the edge of the mating pieces as before, and drill 1/4" holes 1-1/8" deep into the edges at those points. Use glue and dowels to fasten the face and bottom to the side pieces. There should be a 3/4" lip where the drawer face meets the drawer bottom.

8. Cut the drawer stop to the dimension indicated and trim one end if needed. Use the No. 8 screw bit to drill two countersunk holes 8-1/2" apart into the 7/8" face of the strip.

Then use 1- 1/4" screws and glue to fasten it to the underside of the top, 3/4" back from the front edge.

9. Cut the piano hinge to slightly less than the width of the face and mount it barrel-down to the lower edge of the cabinet face. Then slip the completed drawer into place against the stop, and adjust the face so the edges all around are even. Drill the hinge-mounting holes in the cabinet bottom. After the final step, when the finish is dry, mount the hinge leaf permanently.

10. Sand the cabinet, legs, and drawer faces and use the sander to take the sharpness from the edges. You can protect the wood with a coat or two of polyurethane or simply use a finishing tung oil.

anywhere wardrobe

These three units can be built separately or used together. Assembled as a group, the suite is just over 5' wide and replaces a closet, dresser, and chest of drawers. Medium-density fiberboard sheets or carefully groomed plywood are the materials of choice to make this project perfect.

Cut List

Medium-density fiberboard is recommended for this project. A-C plywood can be used if gaps in the exposed edges are filled before finishing.

MIRROR CABINET

1	Top	3/4" X 21-1/2" X 23"
1	Bottom	3/4" X 21-1/2" X 23"
2	Sides	3/4" X 14" X 23"
1	Back	3/4" X 21-1/2" X 56"
1	Divider	3/4" X 1-3/4" X 14"
1	Support	3/4" X 1-3/4" X 21-1/4"
4	Legs (pine)	1-3/4" X 2-3/4" X 19-1/2"
2	Stretchers(pine)	3/4" X 1-3/4" X 19"
1	Brace (pine)	3/4" X 1-3/4" X 16"
4	Drawer sides	3/4" X 11-3/4" X 22-3/4"
4	Drawer ends	3/4" X 8" X 11-3/4"
2	Drawer faces	3/8" X 10-1/2" X 14-3/4"
2	Drawer bottoms	1/4" X 8-3/4" X 22"
1	Mirror	19-1/2" X 39-1/2"

WARDROBE

1	Top	3/4" X 21-1/2" X 23-1/2"
1	Bottom	3/4" X 21-1/2" X 23-1/2"
2	Sides	3/4" X 23-1/2" X 69-1/2"
1	Back	3/16" X 21" X 70-1/2"
4	Legs (pine	1-3/4" X 2-3/4" X 4-3/4"
1	Closet rod	1-1/8" X 20-3/8"

Hardware and Supplies

3" Bin grips
No. 6 X 1" cabinet screws
No. 6 X 1-5/8" cabinet screws
No. 6 X 2" cabinet screws
16-Gauge X 1" brads
16-Gauge X 1-1/2" brads
Mirror clips
3/8" Dowel plugs
Wood filler
Aliphatic resin glue
Latex paint

CHEST OF DRAWERS

1	Top	3/4" X 21-1/2" X 23-1/2"
1	Bottom	3/4" X 21-1/2" X 23-1/2"
2	Sides	3/4" X 23-1/2" X 69-1/2"
1	Back	3/16" X 21" X 70-1/2"
4	Shelves	3/4" X 20" X 23-1/2"
3	Dividers	3/4" X 1-3/4" X 14"
3	Supports	3/4" X 1-3/4" X 21-3/4"
4	Legs (pine)	1-3/4" X 2-3/4" X 4-3/4"
8	Drawer sides	3/4" X 11-3/4" X 22-3/4"
8	Drawer ends	3/4" X 8" X 11-3/4"
4	Drawer faces	3/8" X 10-1/2" X 14-3/4"
4	Drawer bottoms	1/4" X 9" X 22"

Suggested Tools

Table saw
Dado blade (optional)
Taper jig (optional)
Backsaw
3/8" Drill
No. 6 screw bit
Phillips-head driver bit
Brace
Expandable bit
Tape measure
Combination square
Hammer
Nail set
3/8" Chisel
Pipe clamps
Sander

Construction Procedure

1. Cut the top, bottom, back, sides, and support of the mirror cabinet to the sizes indicated. Measure and mark a line longitudinally down the center of the bottom piece. Glue and fasten the support strip on edge over the line so one end is flush with the rear edge of the bottom. Use three No. 6 X 1-5/8" screws driven from the opposite side and spaced 9-1/2" apart.

2. Measure 3/4" from each long edge of the top and bottom pieces and mark a line on the inside faces. Stand the sides between these lines and mark for screw holes, beginning 1" from an end, then spaced 7" apart, four screws along each joint. Use a No. 6 screw bit adjusted for 1-5/8" pilot depth and counterbore slightly below the surface of the panel for later plugging or filling. Glue and fasten the cabinet joints using No. 6 X 1-5/8" cabinet screws.

3. Cut the divider to 14" in length. Fit it vertically at the front of the case and drill mounting holes through the bottom surface and upward at an angle from the face at the top. Apply glue to its ends and the lower edge and fasten it to the top and bottom with No. 6 X 1-5/8" cabinet screws. (Be careful not to penetrate the table top with the point of the screw; use a shorter fastener if necessary.)

4. Cut the four legs to length. Measure 4-3/4" from one end of each leg and make a mark on one of the narrow faces. Then measure 1-5/8" from the opposite narrow face at the end and make a mark on the wide face. Use a backsaw or a taper jig on the table saw to cut from the 4-3/4" point to the 1-5/8" point to create a taper on each leg. Then, from a point 7/8" above the 4-3/4" point, measure inward 1-3/8" and drill a counter-bored hole through the wide leg faces using a No. 6 screw bit. Finally, measure down 7-3/8" from the unta-pered ends of two legs and drill a hole—counterbored 3/4"—through the center of two of the narrow leg faces.

5. Glue and fasten the legs flush with the sides and rear edge of the cabinet, and 1/2" back from the front edge, with tapers facing on each set and the legs with the two holes in the rear. Attach the legs from the top using countersunk No. 6 X 2" cabinet screws spaced diagonally 2-1/4" apart. Cut the two stretchers and the rear brace to fit their places between the legs, hold them in position, and drill pilot holes into their ends using the existing holes in the legs as a guide. Fasten the stretchers and brace using glue and No. 6 X 2" cabinet screws.

6. Mark a line across the rear face of the back piece 3/8" and 15-1/8" from its lower edge. Then beginning at a point 1-1/2" from the lower edge, measure and mark points 4-1/8" apart, stopping before the 15-1/8" line. On the two horizontal lines, mark points beginning 2-1/4" from one side and spaced 5-5/8" apart. Drill countersunk holes at all points, predrill the pilot holes, and fasten the back to the rear edges of the cabinet using No. 6 X 1-5/8" screws. Position the mirror over the face of the back piece and drill mounting holes for the mirror clips, one near each corner.

7. Cut the drawer sides, bottom, front, and back pieces, and the two drawer faces. Measure 1/2" from the lower edges of each drawer side and end and cut a 3/8"-deep, 1/4" groove down the inside face of each piece. Slip the drawer bottoms into the grooves, then apply glue to the side edges of the drawer ends and tack the sides to the edges using 1-1/2" wire brads. Set the heads beneath the surfaces. Round the sharp edges on each of the drawer faces with a sander, and attach them, with the lower edge extending beyond the drawer case by 3/8", to the front of the drawers using glue and two No. 6 X 1" cabinet screws.

8. Fill all the screw holes with wood filler or sections of 3/8" dowel plug glued into the openings. Sand smooth when dry, and sand the sur-face of the legs, the brace, and the stretchers. Paint the cabinet with two coats of interior latex. Secure the mirror by installing the clips then attach the bin handles.

9. The assembly of the chest of drawers follows the same sequence, except that the four shelves must be set in place prior to installing the three dividers and supports. They are fastened from the sides using No. 6 X 1-5/8" cabinet screws counterbored 1/8" beneath the surface and filled with wood filler or dowel sections. All the drawer openings and the shelf directly above are sized equally and to the same dimensions as the mirror cabinet; the drawers are also the same size. The top shelf has an inside height of 10-1/2". The legs are tapered in the same manner, but the taper runs the full length of the leg, or 4-3/4", and they are each secured with screws spaced diagonally 2" apart. The back of the chest and the wardrobe are both secured with a bead of glue and 1" wire brads.

10. The assembly of the wardrobe is exactly the same as that of the chest of drawers, except a 1/2"-deep, 1-1/8" hole is drilled 4-3/4" from the top and 11-3/4" from the front edge of the inner face of each side to hold the closet rod. When making the bore, do not allow the point to penetrate the outer face of the side pieces.

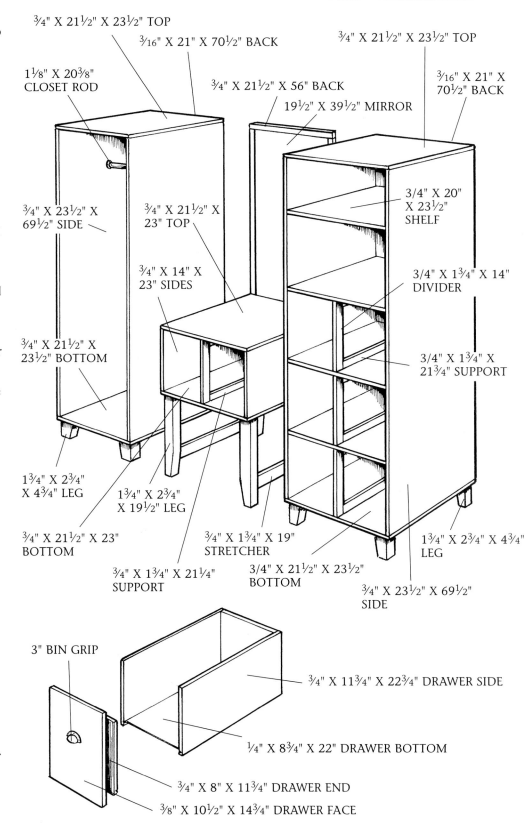

¾" X 21½" X 23½" TOP

³⁄₁₆" X 21" X 70½" BACK

1⅛" X 20⅜" CLOSET ROD

¾" X 21½" X 56" BACK

¾" X 21½" X 23½" TOP

³⁄₁₆" X 21" X 70½" BACK

19½" X 39½" MIRROR

¾" X 23½" X 69½" SIDE

¾" X 21½" X 23" TOP

3/4" X 20" X 23½" SHELF

¾" X 14" X 23" SIDES

3/4" X 1¾" X 14" DIVIDER

¾" X 21½" X 23½" BOTTOM

3/4" X 1¾" X 21¾" SUPPORT

1¾" X 2¾" X 4¾" LEG

1¾" X 2¾" X 19½" LEG

¾" X 21½" X 23" BOTTOM

¾" X 1¾" X 19" STRETCHER

¾" X 21½" X 23½" BOTTOM

1¾" X 2¾" X 4¾" LEG

¾" X 1¾" X 21¼" SUPPORT

¾" X 23½" X 69½" SIDE

3" BIN GRIP

¾" X 11¾" X 22¾" DRAWER SIDE

¼" X 8¾" X 22" DRAWER BOTTOM

¾" X 8" X 11¾" DRAWER END

⅜" X 10½" X 14¾" DRAWER FACE

day bed

Sometimes storage space is not only where you find it, but what you can replace when you get it. This built-in podium bed boasts nine good-sized drawers, two big covered storage bins, and a pair of comfortable sleeping pallets. But it's also a snack table, a work surface, and a great place to hang out.

Suggested Tools

Table saw
Circular saw
Backsaw
Miter box
3/8" Drill
3/16" drill bit
No. 6 screw bit
No. 8 screw bit
Tape measure
Framing square
Combination square
Level
Flat pry bar
Hammer
Nail set
Sander

Hardware and Supplies

No. 6 X 3/4" cabinet screws
No. 8 X 1-1/2" cabinet screws
No. 8 X 1-1/2" cabinet screws
No. 8 X 2" cabinet screws
No. 8 X 2-1/4" cabinet screws
No. 8 X 3-1/2" wood screws
6-Penny finish nails
3/4" Corner braces
22" Drawer slides
1-1/4" Wooden knobs
3" Hand pulls
Aliphatic resin glue
Wood filler
Latex paint

Cut List

Cabinet-grade plywood or medium-density fiberboard is recommended for this project. It's advisable to use plywood and commercial board stock for the framing members.

3	Base strips	3/4" X 2-1/2" X 192"
1	Back strip	3/4" X 5-1/2" X 192"
4	Wall anchors	1" X 1-3/4" X 7"
2	Wall nailers	1-1/2" X 3-1/2" X 92-1/4"
1	Wall nailer	1-1/2" X 3-1/2" X 192"
1	Front header	1-1/2" X 3-1/2" X 192"
11	Stud supports	3/4" X 1" X 10-1/2"
5	Drawer dividers	3/4" X 5-1/2" X 24"
5	Front panel supports	3/4" X 14-3/4" X 24"
5	Rear panel supports	3/4" X 14-3/4" X 22-1/2"
5	Bridge plates	3/4" X 5-1/2" X 53"
1	Platform ledger	1-1/2" X 3-1/2" X 92-1/4"
4	Bed slat ledgers	3/4" X 1-3/4" X 92-1/4"
2	Bed head supports	3/4" X 2-1/2" X 40"
2	Bed head supports	3/4" X 1-3/4" X 40"

4	Hatch ledgers	1-1/2" X 3-1/2" X 46-1/2"
4	Hatch ledgers	1-1/2" X 3-1/2" X 40"
36	Bed slats (hardwood)	3/4" X 1-3/4" X 39-7/8"
4	Bed slat rails	3/4" X 1-3/4" X 77"
1	Face board	3/4" X 4-3/4" X 192"
2	Trim rails	1/2" X 1-3/4" X 96"
1	Trim rail	1/2" X 1-3/4" X 192"
1	False drawer face	3/4" X 7-7/8" X 9-3/4"
9	Drawer faces	3/4" X 9-3/4" X 20-1/4"
18	Drawer sides	3/4" X 7-3/4" X 23-1/2"
18	Drawer ends	3/4" X 7-3/4" X 17-1/8"
9	Drawer bottoms	1/4" X 17-7/8" X 22-3/4"
1	Left-hand platform	3/4" X 21-1/8" X 96"
1	Right-hand platform	3/4" X 7-7/8" X 96"
2	Bed head platforms	3/4" X 15" X 40"
2	Hatch head platforms	3/4" X 22-1/2" X 41-1/2"
2	Hatch foot platforms	3/4" X 25-1/2" X 41-1/2"
2	Hatch covers	3/4" X 41-1/2" X 48"

Construction Procedure

1. The bed podium is shown at 8' X 16' dimensions. To adjust for length to suit your space, the right-hand platform (between the drawer and the wall) can be narrowed or extended as needed. Remove the baseboard from the work area and locate the position of the wall studs on the three wall surfaces you are building against. Mark 16" vertical lines at the stud locations from the floor up. Mark a horizontal line at 14-3/4" from the floor on all three walls.

2. Cut the three wall nailers to length and level them with their upper edges at the horizontal lines. Fasten to the studs with 3-1/2" wood screws. Attach the back nailer first so the side nailers will butt against its face.

3. Cut the front header to fit wall-to-wall. Butt it edge-up against the ends of each side wall nailer and fasten with No. 8 X 2-1/2" cabinet screws.

4. Cut two of the base strips. These 16' pieces do not have to be a continuous length of wood, but shorter pieces should be joined with a mending plate to assure integrity. Screw the rear base strip to the wall at the studs, on edge against the floor, with No. 8 X 2-1/4" cabinet screws. Screw the front base stripflat to the floor with No. 8 X 2" cabinet

screws; its forward edge should be plumb with the forward edge of the front header.

5. Cut the remaining base strip and the back strip. Stand the base strip on edge 22-1/2" forward of the rear wall, and the back strip 24-3/4" behind the face of the frame at the front. Cut the wall anchors and fasten them to the walls at the outer faces of the two strips, except for the forward left-hand one, which gets fastened on its strip's inner face; the anchors may be cut wider if needed to meet the wall studs. Fasten the strips to the edges of the anchors with No. 8 X 1-1/2" screws.

6. Cut the drawer dividers and the front and rear panel supports. On the five rear panel supports, cut 3/4" X 2-1/2" notches in the lower rear corners, and 1-1/2" X 3-1/2" notches in the upper rear corners. On the front panel supports, cut similar notches into the front corners, but adjust the lower notches to match the flat orientation of the front base strip. On the edges opposite the notches on each support, cut 2-1/2"-wide, 5-1/2"-deep notches in the upper corners to hold the bridge plates. Cut 3/4" X 2-1/2" notches in the lower front corners of each drawer divider.

7. Each drawer housing is 19-5/8" in inside width. Use a tape and square to measure and mark the exact locations of each divider and front panel support along the front base strip to fit this schedule, starting from the left-hand side. To eliminate any confusion, mark on both sides of each piece. Cut the 11 stud supports to 10-1/2" or whatever length adjustment is needed to maintain the front header at level. Then, starting at the left- hand wall, fasten a drawer divider between a support stud and the 5-1/2" back strip using two No. 8 X 2" cabinet screws spaced 3-1/2" apart at each joint. First secure the divider to the wall with 2-1/4" screws, then drill and drive the screws into the face of the stud and the back strip. Continue in this manner by fastening a panel support next, then a divider, then a support, and so on, ending with a panel support. The studs can be secured to the panel supports with three screws spaced 2-3/4" apart. At the top of each stud, drill an oblique pilot hole into the front header and drive countersunk 2" cabinet screws into the holes to hold the studs securely; the last stud at the right-hand corner is fastened top and bottom in this way because there is no panel behind it.

8. Measure the positions of the five front panel supports and install the five rear panel supports directly in line with them, using obliquely driven 2" screws at the rear to fasten the panels to the nailers and base

strips. At the front, secure the strip to each panel with two 2" screws spaced 1-1/2" apart. You may add 3/4" corner brackets where needed for additional strength.

9. Cut the five bridge plates and the four bed slat ledgers to length. Slip each plate into position and secure it by fastening a ledger to the inside faces of each bed side so each one's upper edge is 2-1/2" below the edge of the panel assembly. Fasten with glue and No. 8 X 1-1/2" cabinet screws spaced 11" apart. When finished, there should be 40" between the inside faces of the bed sides and 40" between the inside faces of each storage bin. The fifth plate is secured with a platform ledger fastened on the right-hand side with No. 8 X 2-1/4" screws.

10. Cut the two different width head supports, the bed slats, and the bed slat rails. Butt the edge of each 1-3/4" head support against the side of a 2-1/2" head support to make a square corner. Fasten with glue and four No. 8 X 1-1/2" cabinet screws driven from the wider boards' face and spaced 9" apart. Attach each assembly across the edges of the bed ledgers so the faces of the uprights are 15" from the rear wall. Drill through the ends and fasten with countersunk No. 8 X 1-1/2" screws. Then lay two slats edge to edge in the center of the ledgers and space

the rest with gaps about 2-3/4" apart. Place a bed slat rail along each edge so the outer edges are 38" apart. Fasten each joint using glue and countersunk No. 8 X 1-1/2" screws. Repeat with the second set of slats, then flip both assemblies over so the slats are on top.

11. Cut the 2 X 4 hatch ledgers to size. Screw and glue the side pieces into the support panels so their upper edges are flush with the top of the panels and the back ends terminate 23-1/4" from the rear wall. Use No. 8 X 2-1/4" screws spaced 10-7/8" apart to hold them. Butt the sides of the crosswise ledgers to the ends of the ones already in place and fasten them using glue and No. 8 X 3-1/2" wood screws driven obliquely.

12. Install the drawer slides with their lower edges 3/4" above the bottom edges of the front panels and dividers, fronts resting on the base strip. Cut the drawer sides, ends, bottoms, and faces to the dimensions given. Use the table saw to cut a 3/8"-deep, 1/4"-wide dado groove into the inside face of the sides and ends, 1/2" from the bottom edge. Assemble each drawer unit by fitting the bottom into the grooves and fastening the sides to the ends with glue and three No. 8 X 1-1/2" countersunk screws spaced 2- 3/4" apart at each joint. Attach the slide brackets to the lower sides of each drawer and slip the drawers into place. Use glue and four countersunk No. 8 X 1-1/4" screws driven from the inside to fasten the drawer faces over the ends so there's 1/4" or so clearance from the floor and they don't bind at the sides. Trim the face board to 4-3/4" in width and whatever length you require. Fasten it flush to the top of the front header using glue and 6-penny finish nails. Set the heads beneath the wood's surface. Cut the false drawer face to size and nail it in place over the right-hand face opening using toe-nailed 6-penny finish nails. Set the heads.

13. Cut the left- and right-hand side platforms, the bed head platforms, the head and foot hatch platforms, and the hatches to size after double-checking the dimensions on your podium. Use 6- penny finish nails to secure the side platforms and the head and foot pieces to the framing members along the edges. Set the nail heads. Miter-cut the ends of the trim rails and install them along the back and side of the podium using 6-penny finish nails.

14. Mount the 3" hand pulls to the hatches using the hardware provided and drill holes for the 1-1/4" drawer knobs in the center of each face. Install the knobs.

15. Fill all the visible nail and screw holes with wood filler and sand when cured. Sand the surfaces and edges of all the exposed wooden components, and brush on at least two coats of latex paint to match the room decor.

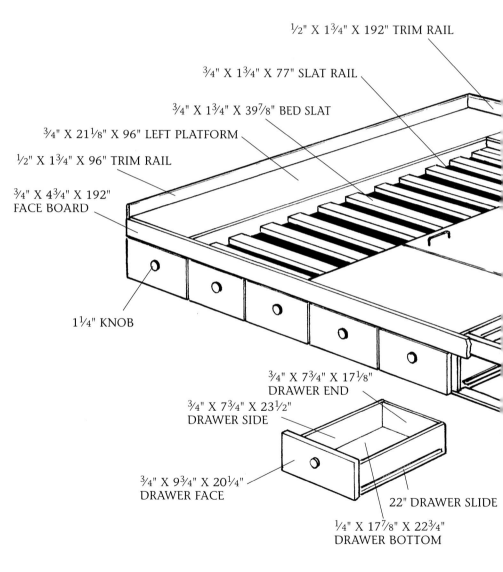

½" X 1¾" X 192" TRIM RAIL

¾" X 1¾" X 77" SLAT RAIL

¾" X 1¾" X 39⅞" BED SLAT

¾" X 21⅛" X 96" LEFT PLATFORM

½" X 1¾" X 96" TRIM RAIL

¾" X 4¾" X 192" FACE BOARD

1¼" KNOB

¾" X 7¾" X 17⅛" DRAWER END

¾" X 7¾" X 23½" DRAWER SIDE

¾" X 9¾" X 20¼" DRAWER FACE

22" DRAWER SLIDE

¼" X 17⅞" X 22¾" DRAWER BOTTOM

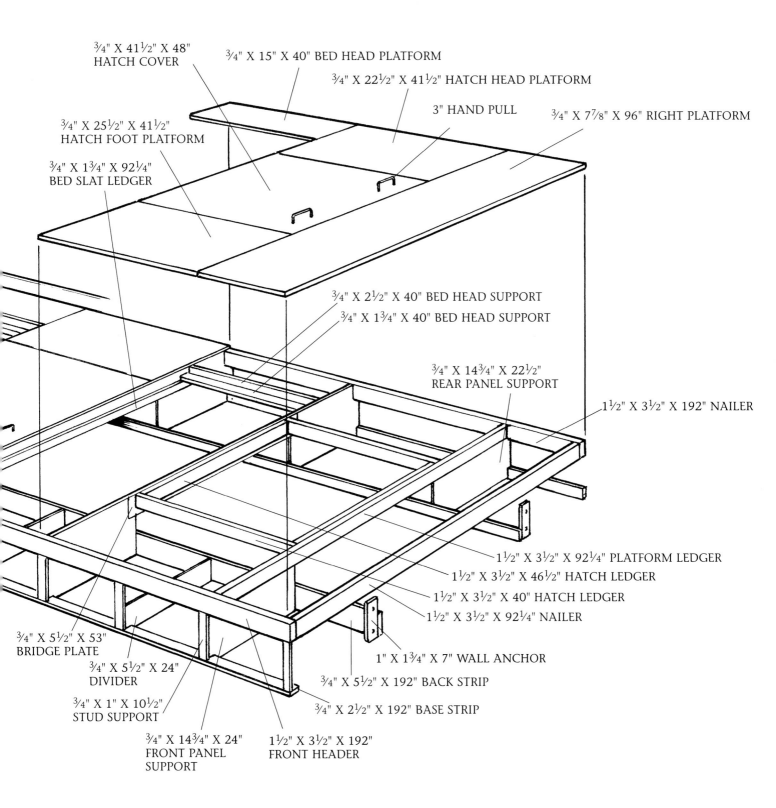

¾" X 41½" X 48" HATCH COVER

¾" X 15" X 40" BED HEAD PLATFORM

¾" X 22½" X 41½" HATCH HEAD PLATFORM

3" HAND PULL

¾" X 7⅞" X 96" RIGHT PLATFORM

¾" X 25½" X 41½" HATCH FOOT PLATFORM

¾" X 1¾" X 92¼" BED SLAT LEDGER

¾" X 2½" X 40" BED HEAD SUPPORT

¾" X 1¾" X 40" BED HEAD SUPPORT

¾" X 14¾" X 22½" REAR PANEL SUPPORT

1½" X 3½" X 192" NAILER

1½" X 3½" X 92¼" PLATFORM LEDGER

1½" X 3½" X 46½" HATCH LEDGER

1½" X 3½" X 40" HATCH LEDGER

1½" X 3½" X 92¼" NAILER

¾" X 5½" X 53" BRIDGE PLATE

¾" X 5½" X 24" DIVIDER

1" X 1¾" X 7" WALL ANCHOR

¾" X 5½" X 192" BACK STRIP

¾" X 2½" X 192" BASE STRIP

¾" X 1" X 10½" STUD SUPPORT

¾" X 14¾" X 24" FRONT PANEL SUPPORT

1½" X 3½" X 192" FRONT HEADER

cousin cabinets, first & second

Simple and functional, these two projects can be built and used individually, or constructed as a matching pair. You even get peg bars to hang your towels on. Its white pine construction can be embellished a bit with the addition of some dowel trim. If you don't care for the dowels, leave them off and simplify your life a little.

Cut List

White pine and textured plywood are recommended for this project. The list specifies materials for the closed cabinet; the open shelf is the same except where noted.

2	Sides	3/4" X 7-1/4" X 34"
1	Back (plywood)	3/4" X 14-1/2" X 36"
4	Shelves (open)	3/4" X 6" X 14-1/2"
2	Top and bottom	3/4" X 6" X 14-1/2"
1	Shelf	3/4" X 5" X 14-1/2"
7	Dowels	1/4" X 15-1/4"
4	Dowels	3/8" X 1-1/2"
2	Door stiles	3/4" X 2" X 27-3/4"
2	Door rails	3/4" X 2" X 10-1/4"
4	Trim	1/2" X 1/2" X 23-3/4"
4	Trim	1/2" X 1/2" X 10-1/4"
1	Obscured glass	10-1/4" X 23-3/4"
1	Peg bar	3/4" X 3" X 16"

Suggested Tools

Table saw
Jigsaw
Backsaw
Miter box
3/8" Drill
No. 6 screw bit
1/16" Drill bit
1/4" Drill bit
3/8" Drill bit
Phillips-head driver bit
Tape measure
Combination square
Marking gauge
Hammer
Nail set
Bar clamps
Sander

Hardware and Supplies

16-Gauge X 2" finish nails
18-Gauge X 1" wire brads
No. 6 X 2-1/2" drywall screws
1-1/2" X 1-3/4" Butt hinges
Magnetic catch
1/4" Pin shelf supports
1" Porcelain knobs
Wood filler
Waterproof aliphatic resin glue
Polyurethane

Construction procedure

1. Cut the two side pieces to 34" in length, then mark the profile as shown on the top and bottom ends of each piece. Cut the shapes with a jigsaw.

2. Cut the back piece to the length indicated and mark its top profile as shown. Cut to shape with a jigsaw.

3. On each side piece, measure 1" down from the top corner, 1" up from the bottom corner, and 3/8" back from the front edge at both locations. Drill a 1/2"-deep 1/4" hole in the inside face. Then measure 16" and 18" up from the lower hole and drill two more holes centered 1-1/4" from the forward edge. Use a square to strike a line through each of those holes to the back edge of the piece and drill two 1/2"-deep, 1/4" holes centered 3-1/2" apart at those lines for the shelf support pins.

4. On the outside face of each side piece, measure 3/4" from the top and bottom corners and draw light pencil lines to the back edge, using a square. Drive three 16-gauge X 2" finish nails 2" apart at each of these lines. Then measure 3/8" from the back edge and draw a line the length of each board. Beginning at a point 1" below the upper corners, drive 2" finish nails 4" apart along each line,

stopping 1" from the lower corners. The nail points should just break the back surface of the wood.

5. Cut two 1/4" dowels to 15-1/4" in length and a third to 15", and glue the longer ones into the 1/4" side sockets at the top and bottom; use the holes at 16" or 18" for the center dowel, but don't glue it—you'll be able to move it later depending on where you want to put the center shelf. Apply a light bead of glue to the ends of the top and bottom piece and slip them between the sides so their front edges meet the top and bottom dowels. Level the pieces, apply glue to their rear edges, and slip the back into place. Adjust the top and bottom to tighten the back joint if needed. Finish driving the nails to secure the joints and set the heads beneath the surface.

6. Cut the door stiles and rails to length. At the end of each rail, measure 3/8" from the front face and 1" from the top edge and drill a 3/8" hole 7/8" deep. Then position the door stiles at the ends of the rails and mark the location of each dowel on the face of its stile. Measure 3/8" in from the marks and drill similar holes into the edge of each stile. Cut four 3/8" dowels to 1-1/2" in length and glue them into the sockets at each door joint. Clamp the door frame until the glue dries.

7. Cut a 45-degree miter into the ends of the shorter trim pieces so they'll fit onto the edges of the door rails. Then cut the stile trim to length so it meets the miters of the rail trim. Drill 1/16" holes about 3-1/2" apart through the inside faces of the rail trim and about 4-1/4" apart on the longer stile trim pieces. Use 1" wire brads to secure one set of trim pieces to the inside edge of the door frame, just off center. Place the glass panel against this trim, then fasten the second set of trim pieces against the opposite side, being careful not to hammer the glass. The trim should protrude slightly from both faces of the door frame.

8. Insert the shelf supports into the side holes and place the center shelf. Then position the door within the frame of the cabinet and mark and drill the position for the two 1-1/2" X 1-3/4" hinges; they should be centered about 4-1/2" from each end of the stile. Center the hole for the 1" knob on the opposite stile and drill.

9. Cut the peg bar to 16" in length and drill four holes for the towel pegs 4" apart down the center, starting 2" from one end.

10. Fill all the nail holes in the cabinet and sand the cabinet and the peg bar. Finish the wood with polyurethane or paint it if desired.

Fasten the door hardware and a magnetic catch, and attach the porcelain knobs to the bar. Fasten the bar 3" or 4" below the cabinet using No. 6 X 2-1/2" screws.

11. When building the open cabinet, note that the shelves are all 6" deep, since there's no door clearance to deal with. The center shelves can be fastened permanently with finish nails or arranged with adjustable pin supports as in the closed cabinet. Remember to keep the face dowels to 15" in length if you plan to make the shelves adjustable.

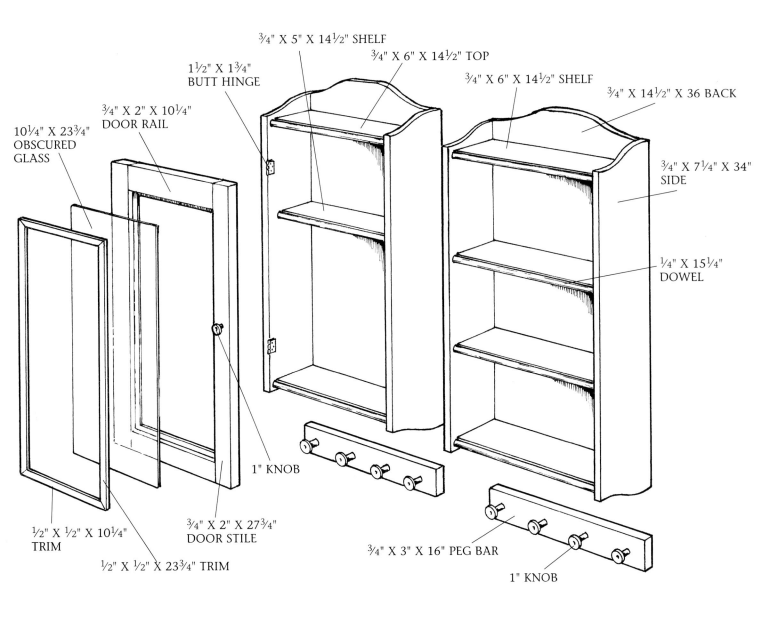

$\frac{3}{4}$" X 5" X 14$\frac{1}{2}$" SHELF

$\frac{3}{4}$" X 6" X 14$\frac{1}{2}$" TOP

1$\frac{1}{2}$" X 1$\frac{3}{4}$" BUTT HINGE

$\frac{3}{4}$" X 6" X 14$\frac{1}{2}$" SHELF

$\frac{3}{4}$" X 2" X 10$\frac{1}{4}$" DOOR RAIL

$\frac{3}{4}$" X 14$\frac{1}{2}$" X 36 BACK

10$\frac{1}{4}$" X 23$\frac{3}{4}$" OBSCURED GLASS

$\frac{3}{4}$" X 7$\frac{1}{4}$" X 34" SIDE

$\frac{1}{4}$" X 15$\frac{1}{4}$" DOWEL

1" KNOB

$\frac{1}{2}$" X $\frac{1}{2}$" X 10$\frac{1}{4}$" TRIM

$\frac{3}{4}$" X 2" X 27$\frac{3}{4}$" DOOR STILE

$\frac{1}{2}$" X $\frac{1}{2}$" X 23$\frac{3}{4}$" TRIM

$\frac{3}{4}$" X 3" X 16" PEG BAR

1" KNOB

mobile bath cabinet

Space in the bathroom is often at a premium, so a cabinet on wheels is a welcome option both in solving storage problems and at cleaning time. With a little imagination, the cabinet can even serve as a kitchen cart, mobile dry bar, or a very compact entertainment center.

Suggested Tools

Table saw
3/8" Drill
1/4" Drill bit
3/8" Forstner bit (optional)
Phillips-head driver bit
Combination square
Marking gauge
Tape measure
Hammer
Nail set
Sander

Hardware and Supplies

16-Gauge X 2" finish nails
18" Towel bar
1/4" X 20-1/2" Threaded rod & nuts
1/2" X 18-1/2" PVC pipe
2-1/2" Casters
3/8" X 1-1/4" Dowels (optional)
Wood filler
Waterproof aliphatic resin
Stain
Polyurethane

Cut List

Cabinet-grade plywood is recommended for this project.

2	Sides	3/4" X 20" X 48"
1	Back	3/4" X 18-1/2" X 48"
4	Shelves	3/4" X 18-1/2"X 18-1/2"
4	Faces	3/4" X 3" X 18-1/2"

Construction Procedure

1. You have the option of joining the cabinet the easy way—with finish nails—or using a more difficult but craftsman-like dowel-joining technique. With either method, the water-resistant glue will hold the case together securely.

2. Cut the sides, back, and the four shelves on the table saw. On the back face of both side pieces, measure from one end, which is the top, and mark horizontal lines at these points: 2-5/8", 17-5/8", 32-5/8", and 47-5/8". Repeat the procedure on the good face, but mark lightly in pencil. Drive 2" finish nails along these lines into the face of the panels 5-1/2" apart, starting 1-3/4" from the rear edge. Then measure in 3/8" from the rear edge and mark a line lightly down the good face of both side pieces. Drive 2" finish nails every 5-3/4" along this line, starting 1" from the top. The points of the nails should just break the back surface of the wood.

3. Run a thin bead of glue along the edges of the back piece, then lay the back, good face down, on a flat work surface and carefully nail the sides into the edges of the back panel, with the top and bottom edges flush. Set the nail heads beneath the surface.

4. Apply a bead of glue to three edges of each of the four shelves and slip them into position at the marked lines by slightly spreading the side pieces and pushing the boards firmly against the back. The plywood's good face should be up, with the grain running in the same direction. Nail the sides to the shelves and set the heads beneath the surface. Measure down from the top of the back piece using the dimensions given earlier and drive 2" finish nails into the rear edge of each shelf starting 1-3/4" from the side and spacing them 5-1/2" apart. Set the heads.

5. Lightly mark a line top to bottom 3/8" from the front edge of the case. Apply glue to the ends and lower rear surface of each face piece and nail them individually to the front of the shelves. The end nails should be spaced 2" apart, and the face nails spaced 5-1/2" apart, starting 1-3/4" from the sides. You can mark a horizontal line 3/8" from the bottom of each face if it would help to keep the nail course straight. Set the heads beneath the surface of the wood.

6. Measure 7" from the lower edge of each side and drill a 1/4" hole 3/8" from the front edge of the cabinet. Fit the towel bar 3-1/2" below the top edge of one side and drill for mounting. Do not install the hardware yet.

7. Fill all the nail holes with wood filler and allow to dry. Sand the inside and outside of the cabinet. Stain the wood to color if desired, then finish the entire cabinet and shelves with two coats of polyurethane.

8. Fasten the casters to the bottom of the case, recessed 3/4" back from each corner, using the hardware provided. Cut the PVC pipe to slip between the cabinet sides and push the 1/4" threaded rod through one side of the cabinet and the pipe until it protrudes from the opposite side. Fasten the rod with stainless steel nuts at both ends. Attach the towel bar using the hardware provided.

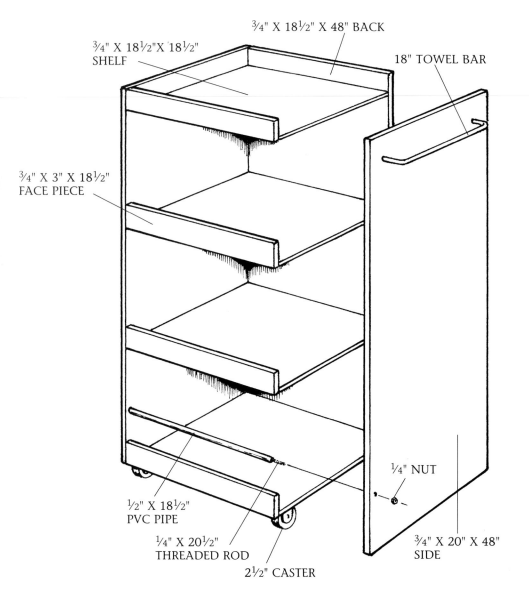

3/4" X 18½" X 48" BACK

3/4" X 18½"X 18½" SHELF

18" TOWEL BAR

3/4" X 3" X 18½" FACE PIECE

¼" NUT

½" X 18½" PVC PIPE

¼" X 20½" THREADED ROD

2½" CASTER

3/4" X 20" X 48" SIDE

bath valet

Dry storage is always welcome in a humid bathroom. This barbershop valet takes up only a 12" X 12" space but provides plenty of room for towels and toiletries. Its light color and obscured glass panels give it a very traditional look that's at home in almost any house.

Suggested Tools

Table saw

Taper jig (optional)

Backsaw

3/8" Drill

No. 6 screw bit

No. 8 screw bit

Phillips-head driver bit

Tape measure

Combination square

Hammer

Nail set

Pipe clamps

Sander

Hardware and Supplies

No. 6 X 1-1/2" cabinet screws

No. 8 X 2" cabinet screws

16-Gauge X 1" brads

1" Knobs

Surface-mount hinges

Magnetic catches

9" Towel rack

Wood filler

Silicone sealant

Waterproof aliphatic resin glue

Latex paint

Cut List

White pine or poplar is recommended for this project.

2	Sides	3/4" X 11-1/4" X 45"
1	Top	3/4" X 10-1/2" X 11-1/4"
1	Bottom	3/4" X 10-1/2" X 11-1/4"
2	Shelves	3/4" X 10-1/2" X 11"
6	Door stiles	3/4" X 2-1/4" X 15"
6	Door rails	3/4" X 2-1/4" X 7-1/2"
4	Legs	2" X 2" X 4-3/4"
1	Back (plywood)	1/4" X 11-1/4" X 44-1/4"
12	Splines (hardboard)	1/8" X 3/4" X 2"
1	Obscured glass	8" X 11"

Construction Procedure

1. Cut the sides, shelves, top, and bottom pieces. Using the table saw, cut a 3/8" rabbet, 1/4" deep, into the rear inner edge of the sides, top, and bottom pieces.

2. From the top edge, measure and mark these points along the side pieces: 3/8", 15-1/8", 29-7/8", and 44-5/8". Strike a line across each board at those points. Using a No. 6 screw bit drill two holes, countersunk 1/8" beneath the surface of the wood, 8-3/4" apart on the lines, measuring back 1-1/4" from the forward edge.

3. Apply a thin strip of glue to the side edges of each shelf and the top and bottom pieces. Lightly clamp the sides to the four pieces, with the cabinet face down on a flat work surface and the horizontal pieces in position over their respective holes. Make sure the top and bottom rabbets are facing inward and the two shelves are pushed all the way down. Drive the 16 No. 6 X 1-1/2" wood screws into the holes.

4. Remove the clamps and trim the plywood back piece to fit within the relief formed by the rabbets. Secure the back with 1" brads spaced 3-1/2" apart all around.

5. Cut the leg pieces to 2" X 2" square, and 4-3/4" in length. Each leg tapers to a 1" X 1" base, so you should mark the taper- cut lines on each face of the legs and make the cuts with a backsaw, or set up a taper jig on your table saw fence to guide the wood through past the blade at the desired angle. Since these pieces are short, be sure to use a push stick when cutting and keep the blade guard in place for safety. Mount one leg to each corner of the cabinet, recessed 3/4" from the sides and faces. Use two No. 8 X 2" screws set diagonally through the upper surface of the bottom panel and spaced 1-3/4" apart.

6. Cut the door rails and stiles. Use the table saw to cut a 1/8" X 3/8" dado into the inner edge of each stile, directly down the center. Then cut a similar dado into the end of each rail piece. Cut a scrap piece of 1/8" hardboard into twelve 3/4" X 2" splines. Dry fit the doors together with one of these splines at each joint; if the door pieces join with a gap, sand the edges of the spline slightly.

7. Lay a thin bead of silicone into only the middle area of two rails and two stiles. Apply the wood glue to two of the splines and fit them to the ends of one stile along with one edge of a glass pane between. Slip the top and bottom rails into position, with the glass captured in the dadoes, then glue the remaining two splines to the ends of the rails and stiles. Clamp the two stiles together. Repeat the procedure to assemble the remaining two doors.

8. Hang the completed doors over the shelf openings using inside surface-mounted hinges. Allow at least 1/8" between each door for clearance to prevent binding. Center the 1" knobs over the unhinged stiles, mark, and drill for mounting. Mark and drill mounting holes for a towel bar, placed 1-1/2" below the upper edge on side.

9. Fill all the screw holes and sand. Paint the cabinet and shelves in the color desired. Install the knobs and towel bar once the paint has dried. If you do not wish to use self-closing hinges, a small magnetic catch can be installed at each knob stile to keep the door closed.

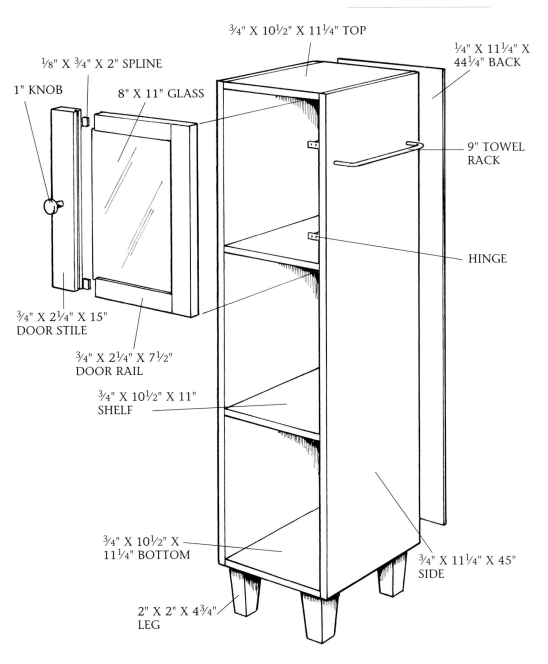

¾" X 10½" X 11¼" TOP

¼" X 11¼" X 44¼" BACK

⅛" X ¾" X 2" SPLINE

1" KNOB

8" X 11" GLASS

9" TOWEL RACK

HINGE

¾" X 2¼" X 15" DOOR STILE

¾" X 2¼" X 7½" DOOR RAIL

¾" X 10½" X 11" SHELF

¾" X 10½" X 11¼" BOTTOM

¾" X 11¼" X 45" SIDE

2" X 2" X 4¾" LEG

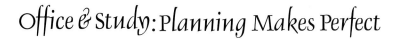

flats rack

You don't have to be an artist to appreciate the practicality of this poster rack. It's designed to hold flats, prints, posters, picture frames and things that don't fit elsewhere easily. Yet the standing bin has only a 3' by 4' footprint and lets you see at a glance what's in store. With a few basic tools and some free time, you'll be able to bolt together a rack of your own in no time flat.

Suggested Tools

Table saw
Backsaw
3/8" Drill
1/4" Drill bit
No. 8 screw bit
Phillips-head driver bit
Try square
Marking gauge
Tape measure
C clamps

Hardware and Supplies

1/4" X 3-1/2" Carriage bolts
No. 8 X 1-1/2" flathead screws
Aliphatic resin glue

Construction Procedure

1. Set the table-saw fence to rip a 1-3/4" dimension. Cut all the pieces requiring a 1-3/4" width to that dimension.

2. Cut one base, one leg brace, and two legs to the lengths indicated.

Cut List

Pine or any straight-grained softwood and A-C interior plywood are recommended for this project.

4	Uprights	1-1/2" X 1-3/4" X 49-1/4"
2	Upright braces	1-1/2" X 1-3/4" X 19"
2	Leg bases	1-1/2" X 1-3/4" X 34-1/4"
2	Leg braces	1-1/2" X 1-3/4" X 21-1/4"
4	Legs	1-1/2" X 1-3/4" X 17-3/4"
12	Slats	3/4" X 1-3/4" X 47-1/4"
1	Bottom	3/4" X 15-3/4" X 47-1/4"

Mark the midpoints of the base and leg brace, and place those pieces parallel to one another on a flat surface with their outer edges 16-1/8" apart and the midpoints aligned.

3. Lay the legs at the ends of the two pieces to form a trapezoid. Use a pencil to mark the outline of the two legs on the surface of both parallel pieces. Mark the underside of the legs where they meet the base and leg brace.

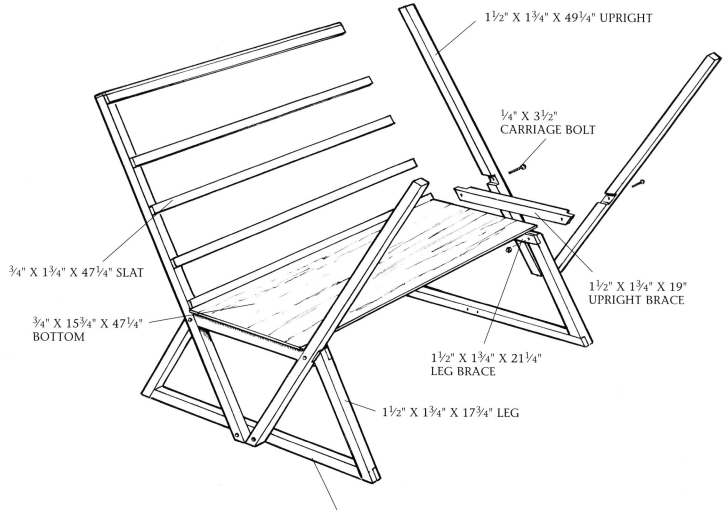

1½" X 1¾" X 49¼" UPRIGHT

¼" X 3½"
CARRIAGE BOLT

¾" X 1¾" X 47¼" SLAT

1½" X 1¾" X 19"
UPRIGHT BRACE

¾" X 15¾" X 47¼"
BOTTOM

1½" X 1¾" X 21¼"
LEG BRACE

1½" X 1¾" X 17¾" LEG

1½" X 1¾" X 34¼" LEG BASE

4. Trim off the corner ends of the base and leg brace at the marked line with a backsaw. Trim off the corner ends of both legs where marked.

5. Use a marking gauge or straightedge to mark the midpoint, in the thickness dimension, of each joint, on both sides and the ends. Connect the outline marks previously made on the wood to the midpoint lines by striking a line along a try square held against the long edge of each piece.

6. Use a backsaw to cut the half-lap joints by removing the waste from each part of the joint. Be careful to check before cutting to be sure you're removing the correct side of each joint. Refer to page 48 for detailed instructions on "How to Cut a Half-Lap Joint" if you need extra guidance. Repeat the procedure described in Steps 2 through 6 to make the remaining legs, base, and brace.

7. Cut the four uprights to 49-1/4" in length. Dry-fit one of the leg assemblies on a flat surface and lay two uprights over it in a "V" pattern, with the joint of the "V" centered over the midpoint of the brace and the outer edge of the uprights flush with the upper corners of the leg assembly. Place one of the upright braces against the uprights so it's

aligned with the leg brace beneath it. Mark its edges on both uprights, mark the edges of the uprights on the brace from below, and mark a line where the lower tips of the uprights extend beyond the base.

8. Use a marking gauge to mark the midpoint of the half-lap joints that will connect the brace with the uprights. Follow the previous procedure for cutting half-lap joints with a backsaw, and trim the corners from the braces and uprights at the marked lines. Repeat the marking and cutting procedure to make the other upright and brace assembly.

9. Align one upright assembly over one of the leg assemblies, with the upright brace against the leg brace. Drill 1/4" holes at the four points shown in the illustration: two at the bottom of the uprights and one each through the uprights and leg assemblies behind them. Fasten the joints with 1/4" X 3-1/2" carriage bolts and glue. Repeat on the second set of upright and leg assemblies.

10. Cut all 12 slats to 47-1/4" in length. Stand the two end assemblies 4' apart and clamp a slat to the end of each set of uprights so its edge extends 3/4" beyond the ends. The ends of the slats should be flush with the edges of the uprights. Use a No. 8 screw bit to drill 1-1/2"-deep holes through the slats and into the wood

behind them. Fasten with glue and one No. 8 X 1-1/2" flathead screw at each joint.

11. Cut the plywood bottom to the dimensions indicated. Place it best side up, and with its ends flush with each upright brace, and use a No. 8 screw bit to drill five 1-1/2"-deep holes, spaced 4" apart, through the bottom and into the brace below at each end. Fasten with No. 8 X 1-1/2" flathead screws.

12. Drill and fasten the remaining ten slats with glue and No. 8 screws. Place the lower slats against the plywood bottom and the cap slats against the ones already in place at the ends of the uprights. The remaining three slats on each side should be centered between the upper and lower set and placed with their edges 4-3/4" apart.

13. Sand the wood lightly and apply an undercoat sealer. Paint the rack in the color of your choice. If the plywood has an attractive grain, you can stain the wood instead of painting it and then coat it with polyurethane.

bookcase worktable

A real space-saver in cramped quarters, this worktable folds up neatly—legs and all—into a functional bookcase when not in use. Made with lumberyard pine or a good-quality plywood, the 5-shelf case is only 30" wide and 12" deep, and stands a reasonable 6' in height. When used as a work table, it occupies another 30" of floor space. The one in the photo has a decoupage finish made from cut magazine pages; it's covered with several coats of polyurethane.

Suggested Tools

Table saw

3/8" Drill

No. 8 Screw bit

Phillips-head driver bit

1/4" Drill bit

5/8" Forstner bit

Tape measure

Combination square

Level

Pipe clamps

Hardware and Supplies

1-1/4" X 1-1/2"

Butt hinges

No. 8 X 2" wood screws

16-Gauge X 1" brads

1/4" Pin shelf supports

Magnetic catch

Aliphatic resin glue

Wood filler

Latex paint

Polyurethane

Cut List

White pine and A-C plywood or medium-density fiberboard, are recommended for this project.

2	Sides	3/4" X 11-1/4" X 72"
1	Top	3/4" X 11" X 28-1/2"
5	Shelves	3/4" X 11" X 28-1/2"
1	Ledger	3/4" X 7" X 28-1/2"
1	Back (hardboard)	1/4" X 29-1/4" X 69"
1	Toe board	3/4" X 3" X 28-1/2"
1	Tabletop	3/4" X 28-1/2" X 29-1/2"
2	Supports	3/4" X 1-3/4" X 28"
2	Baluster legs	1-3/4" X 28-1/2"
2	Dowels	5/8" X 23-1/2"
2	Dowels	5/8" X 1-1/2"

Construction Procedure

1. Cut the two side pieces, and cut 1/4"-deep X 1/2" rabbets into each inside rear edge. Then, starting from one end, mark lines with a square across each board at the following points: 3/8", 11", 24", 38", and 68-5/8". Use a No. 8 screw bit to counterbore three holes 3-1/4" apart along each of these line. Drill from the best face of the wood.

2. Butt the sides against the ends of the shelves and center the top and four of the shelf pieces over each line of holes with the rear edges flush to

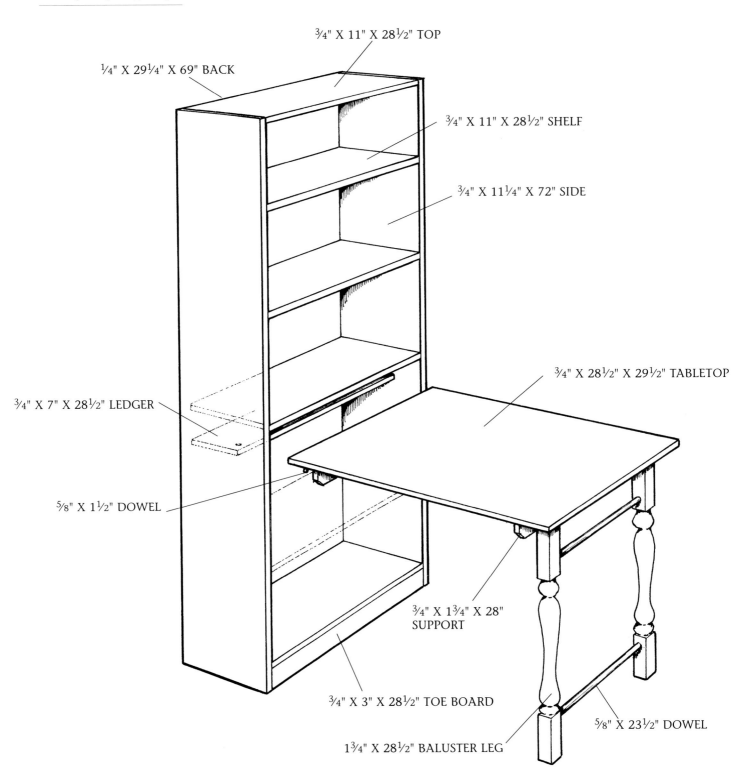

¾" X 11" X 28½" TOP

¼" X 29¼" X 69" BACK

¾" X 11" X 28½" SHELF

¾" X 11¼" X 72" SIDE

¾" X 28½" X 29½" TABLETOP

¾" X 7" X 28½" LEDGER

⅝" X 1½" DOWEL

¾" X 1¾" X 28" SUPPORT

¾" X 3" X 28½" TOE BOARD

⅝" X 23½" DOWEL

1¾" X 28½" BALUSTER LEG

the inside of the rabbets. Clamp temporarily and redrill the holes with the drill stop set at a 2" depth to make pilot holes in the ends of the five horizontal boards. Glue and fasten each joint using No. 8 X 2" wood screws.

3. Cut the toe board to fit and attach it just beneath the lowest shelf using glue and No. 8 X 2" screws drilled and fastened as the shelves were.

4. Drill two 5/8" holes through the ledger board, each centered 2" from the side and 2" from one edge.

5. Cut the tabletop to fit the opening above the bottom shelf. There should be at least 1/4" clearance at the upper edge and about 1/8" along the vertical edges to prevent binding.

6. Cut the two supports. Trim their ends to a 45-degree angle, starting about 1/2" down from the upper edge. Use the No. 8 screw bit to bore three holes through the lower edge of each support, one in the center and the other two 12" to each side. Countersink the openings.

7. Center the two supports on the back face of the tabletop between the side edges, and place them 2-1/2" from the top and bottom edges. Drill 1/2"-deep pilot holes into the top and

fasten the supports with No. 8 X 2" screws.

8. Lay the two legs side by side and mark points 4" from the top and bottom ends on the faces. Drill 5/8" holes, 1/2"-deep, at each point. Fasten the legs together by gluing a 23-1/2" dowel into each set of sockets, and lay the assembly on a flat surface to dry. Once it's rigid, center and fasten it to the outside face of one of the supports, using one 1-1/4" butt hinge per leg and the hardware provided.

9. Set the bookcase in an upright position and tack the back in place using 16-gauge X 1" brads. Place the tabletop, with legs extended, between the sides. Level the top and mark the point where its underneath, or back face, meets each side. Fasten the ledger board between the sides and against the back of the bookcase with its upper surface at the marked points, using No. 8 X 2" screws, making sure the 5/8" holes are toward the front.

10. Reposition the table and mark the outline of each 5/8" ledger hole on its bottom surface. Drill a 5/8"-deep, 5/8" socket into the table back at those points with a Forstner bit, being careful not to penetrate the good face. Bevel one edge of each 5/8" X 1-1/2" dowel and glue the unbeveled ends into the sockets.

11. Locate the removable shelf at the desired level between the lowest shelf and the ledger board. Drill a pair of 1/4" holes 8" apart into each side of the cabinet without penetrating the wood completely. Insert the pin shelf supports and install the shelf. (This shelf must be removed and stored in the case in order to close the table door.)

12. Fold up the legs and place the tabletop vertically into its opening. To keep it from falling open, you may want to fasten a magnetic catch at the lower edge of the middle shelf and attach the metal catch plate to the underside of the tabletop.

13. Fill all the exposed screw holes and sand the wood. Finish the cabinet, shelves, and table as desired. The bookcase in the photo has a decoupage lining and work surface, which has been covered with polyurethane.

cubbyhole desk

A modern panel-and-cubby desk that's easily made to fit any space. This clean design eliminates drawers and back altogether. The crisp look comes about from the use of biscuit or wafer joints, which are internal and completely hidden from view once the unit is assembled. No biscuit joiner? If you're careful to measure accurately, you can duplicate the task with 3/8" dowels, which are functional but not nearly as sturdy.

Suggested Tools

Table saw
Circular saw (optional)
Biscuit joiner
Tape measure
Combination square
Straightedge
Pipe clamps

Hardware and Supplies

No. 10 biscuits
Stain
Varnish or polyurethane

Construction Procedure

1. The two large-panel cuts for the top and shelf must be done accurately. You may prefer to use a clamped-on fence and a circular saw rather than a table saw to make these cuts. If your lumber supplier has a large panel saw, it may be worthwhile for you to have those two pieces custom-cut at purchase.

Cut List

Cabinet-grade plywood or veneer-faced medium density fiberboard is recommended for this project.

1	Top	3/4" X 24" X 84"
1	Shelf	3/4" X 24" X 84"
10	Dividers	3/4" X 4" X 24"
4	Sides	3/4" X 20-3/4" X 24"
2	Bottoms	3/4" X 5-1/2" X 24"
4	Pedestal sides	3/4" X 2-1/2" X 21"
4	Pedestal ends	3/4" X 2-1/2" X 3-1/2"

2. Once the panels are cut, lay one, back face up, on a flat surface. Use a combination square or marking gauge to mark a series of points, about 11" apart, 3/8" from the edge at each end. Then measure in 5-1/8" from each end and make a second series of marks; measure in 17-7/8" and make a third series; measure in 30-5/8" and make a final series of marks. Strike a pencil line through each of these sets of points using a staightedge. Repeat this procedure on the second, or shelf, panel, but

this time with the good face up. Lay the panels side by side to check that there are eight lines in the same position on both.

3. Turn the shelf panel over so its back face is up. Measure and strike another set of four lines on this face using the first two—3/8" and 5-1/8"—dimensions as before. Then mark cross-lines at points 3-1/2" and 9" in from each edge on these lines.

4. Cut the ten divider pieces on the table saw. Measure 3/8" from the side, and strike lines down the center of the 24" edges of each piece. Mark cross-lines at points 2" in from each end and at 12" on both edges of all the pieces.

5. Lay the shelf panel good face up and mark cross-lines at points 2" in from each edge and at 12" on each of the eight lines drawn on the surface, to match those made on the dividers. Then lay the top panel back face up and repeat the same procedure.

6. At each of the cross points on the dividers, carefully cut slots with the biscuit joiner to match the No. 10 biscuits or "wafers." Then use the tool to cut into the back face of the top panel and the good face of the shelf panel at their respective marked cross-points. Exact alignment of the tool fence with the marks is essential for a good joint.

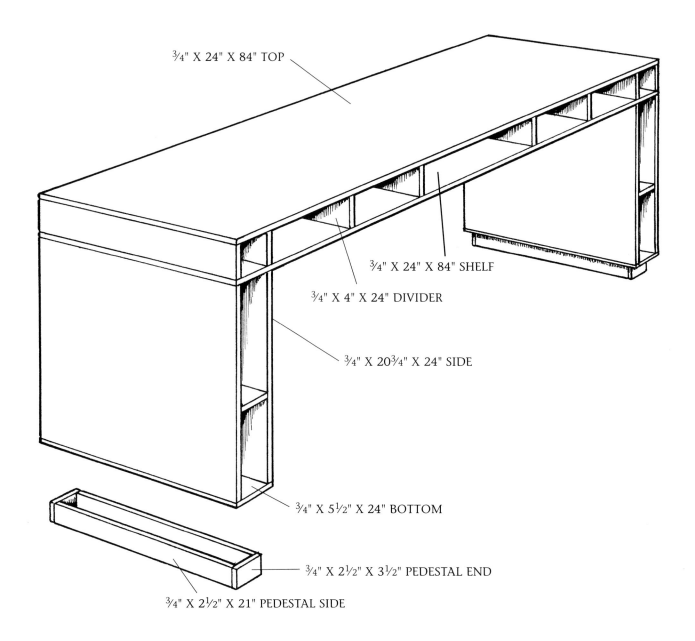

¾" X 24" X 84" TOP

¾" X 24" X 84" SHELF

¾" X 4" X 24" DIVIDER

¾" X 20¾" X 24" SIDE

¾" X 5½" X 24" BOTTOM

¾" X 2½" X 3½" PEDESTAL END

¾" X 2½" X 21" PEDESTAL SIDE

7. Dry-fit 24 wafers into the upper face of the shelf, try the eight dividers for fit, then place the top panel. For difficult fits, you may have to sand the edges of the wafer to increase its edge taper slighty. Apply glue to the lower set of wafers, insert the dividers, then glue the upper wafer set. Fit the top with the help of a friend, and clamp the entire assembly together along both edges.

8. Cut the sides, bottoms, and pedestal pieces. On the back, or inside, face of each side piece measure 10-3/8" from the upper end and strike a line across the face. Mark cross-lines at 2" in from each edge, and at 12", along each line. Then strike lines down the center of each 24" end and mark cross-lines at 3-1/2" and 9" from the edges on each of the upper ends. The lower ends should be cross-marked at 2" and 12" from the edges.

9. Lay the two bottom pieces good face up. Measure in 3/8" from each long edge and strike a line the length of the wood. Mark cross-lines at 2" in, and 12", from the edges. Turn the two pieces back face up and measure in 1-3/8" from the edges on each piece. Strike lines along the length. Measure cross-lines at 4" in from the ends and 12" on each line. Use the biscuit joiner set for No. 10 wafers to cut slots at each cross-point on the sides and bottom piece.

10. Dry-fit the wafers and pieces for fit, then glue and clamp each leg assembly and allow to dry. In the meantime, strike a line down the center of one long edge and the two ends of each pedestal side. Mark cross-lines at 2-1/2" in and 10-1/2" from the ends along the 21" lines, and at 1-1/4" from the edge at each end. Make corresponding marks on the back side of each of the four pedestal ends. Cut the slots with the biscuit joiner.

11. Fit and glue each pedestal assembly together with wafers and

clamp it. Once the glue has dried, fit the pedestals to the legs with wafers and clamp them in place. Finally, with those joints cured, glue each leg assembly in place, with wafers, beneath the shelf panel, using the slots you cut earlier. Allow to dry for 24 hours.

12. Stain and finish the desk as desired. A coat of lacquer or polyurethane will protect the surface of the wood somewhat from scratches.

sun shelf

We all want a spot to put our favorite plants and herbs when they can't be out-doors. A sunny windowsill is the perfect place, and this four-platform shelf puts the entire window to use.

Suggested Tools

Table saw
3/8" Drill
No. 6 screw bit
1/8" Drill bit
Pliers
Combination square
Tape measure

Cut List

White pine or medium-density fiberboard is recommended for this project.

2 Sides   3/4" X 7-1/4" X 48"
5 Shelves 3/4" X 7-1/4" X 29-1/2"

Hardware and Supplies

1/2" X 2-1/2" Corner plates
No. 6 X 2" Cabinet screws
3/8" Wooden plugs
11-Gauge hook-and-eye sets
Aliphatic resin glue

Construction Procedure

1.   Measure the inside dimensions of your window in case you need to adjust the size of the shelf. If the sash framing isn't deep enough, you can rest the forward portion of the shelf on a table or bookshelf that matches the height of your window-sill. With windows taller or shorter than 54", the mid shelves will have to be spaced accordingly.

2.   Rip the sides and shelves to width on the table saw. Then cut to length. Cut the two sides and five shelves to the appropriate length to fit your window opening.

3. Measure 3/8" in from each end of the side pieces and mark a line across the wood. Measure between the lines, subtract 3/4", and divide that dimension by 4. (On a 48" board, the result would be 11-5/8".) Starting 3/8" below the first line, make a line at whatever points you came up with for your window. This procedure will allow you to space the mid shelves evenly.

4. Drill two counterbored holes spaced 5" apart at each line using the No. 6 screw bit. Recess the entry holes slightly to provide a socket for the wooden plugs that you'll add later.

5. Place one shelf board at each end of the side pieces to form a rectangular box. The sides should butt against the ends of the shelves. Fasten the top and bottom pieces using No. 6 X 2" cabinet screws. Position a 1/2" X 2-1/2" corner plate at each corner and fasten it to the rear edges using the plate hardware provided.

6. Place the remaining three shelf boards at the lines you just made. Fasten them using No. 6 X 2" screws.

7. Cover all the screw holes by gluing 3/8" wooden plugs into the openings. Sand the wood and paint as desired.

8. Position the completed shelf in the window. For safety from tipping, locate a spot on each side near the top where you can inconspicu-ously fasten a small hook-and-eye set. Use a 1/8" drill bit to fasten eye screws to the window frame and the hooks to the sides of the shelf.

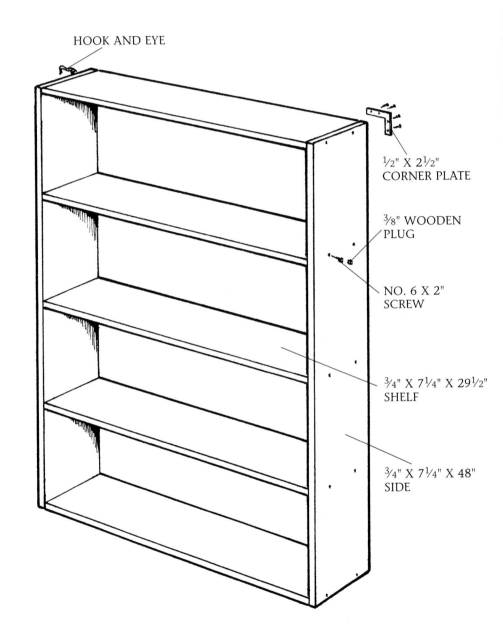

HOOK AND EYE

$\frac{1}{2}$" X $2\frac{1}{2}$"
CORNER PLATE

$\frac{3}{8}$" WOODEN PLUG

NO. 6 X 2"
SCREW

$\frac{3}{4}$" X $7\frac{1}{4}$" X $29\frac{1}{2}$"
SHELF

$\frac{3}{4}$" X $7\frac{1}{4}$" X 48"
SIDE

ceiling nook

For houses with a peaked attic roof or an unfinished cathedral ceiling, this minor addition will set you up with a long narrow space to store those awkward seasonal items that won't easily fit elsewhere.

Cut List

White pine is recommended for this project.

3	Face frame	3/4" X 2-1/4" X 20"
3	Inner frame	3/4" X 1-1/2" X 19-1/4"
3	Strips	3/8" X 3/8" X 18-3/4"
1	Acrylic panel	19" X 19" X 19"
2	Stops	1/2" X 1-1/4"
2	Floor	1/2" X 12" X length as required

Suggested Tools

Table saw
Circular saw
Backsaw
Miter box
3/8" Drill
1/8" Drill bit
No. 6 screw bit
Phillips-head driver bit
Hammer
Nail set
Tape measure

Hardware and Supplies

Magnetic catch
1-1/4" X 2" Butt hinges
No. 6 X 1-1/4" wood screws
16-Gauge X 1" brads
1" Wooden knob
Aliphatic resin glue
Latex paint

Construction Procedure

1. Measure the distance along the top of the collar tie between the rafters. With a finished ceiling, you will have to remove the ceiling panel in order to nail a collar tie to the rafters at the front and back of the shelf you're about to build. If you plan on storing long items such as skis or rigid tent poles, measure from the roof gable, or wall, forward to the nearest set of rafters in order to place the tie at a location that will provide enough room to hold the items.

2. Rip the face frame material to 2-1/4" in width, and cut the lower piece, to start, to the same dimension as the span of the collar tie you just measured. Trim one end to match the existing angle of the ceiling, then retrim the other to allow for the opposite ceiling angle minus the 2-1/4" width of the adjoining face frame. Repeat for the second and third leg until the entire triangle frame is complete.

3. Lay the frame members down on a flat surface with the ends butted together. Cut the three 3/4" X 1-1/2" inner frame pieces to fit 1/4" from the inside edges of the face frame. (One end of each inner frame piece must overlap the joint of the face frame beneath it.) Fasten the inner frame to the back of the face frame with glue and three No. 6 X 1-1/4" wood screws per length. The end screws should penetrate the adjoining face piece. Fit the completed frame assembly in place and trim the corners or edges if needed.

4. Cut a piece of acrylic panel to fit between the inside edges of the inner frame. Set it in place, then trim three 3/8" X 3/8" strips to fit along the exposed portion of the frame and the edges of the glazing. Secure the strips with 1" brads.

5. Cut two stops to fit along the inside of the ceiling if the rafters don't already form stops. Fasten them with No. 6 X 1-1/4" countersunk wood screws. Lay the frame assembly against the edge of the collar tie and mark the position for two butt hinges spaced 18" apart. Fasten to the frame and tie using the hardware provided.

6. Set each floor half in place and secure with 1" brads set flush with the surface. Paint the framing and trim, then install the wooden knob and magnetic catch.

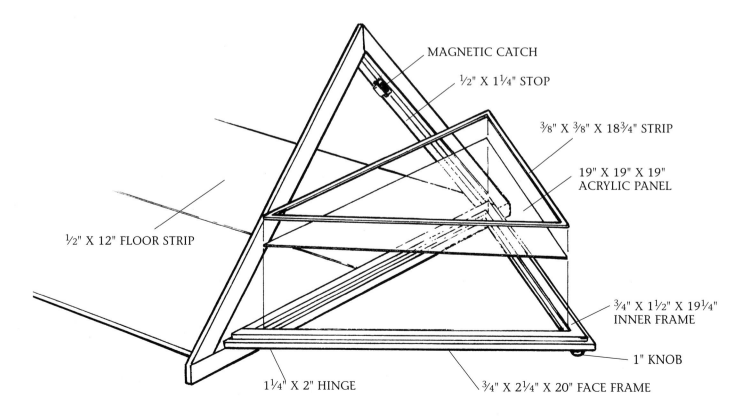

MAGNETIC CATCH

½" X 1¼" STOP

⅜" X ⅜" X 18¾" STRIP

19" X 19" X 19" ACRYLIC PANEL

½" X 12" FLOOR STRIP

¾" X 1½" X 19¼" INNER FRAME

1" KNOB

1¼" X 2" HINGE

¾" X 2¼" X 20" FACE FRAME

stair trap

Not everyone has a stair landing, and some landings can't easily be modified. But if you're up for a small remodeling challenge, you might be interested in this storage idea that'll give you a very utilitarian 3' X 4' (more or less) hiding space under the steps, accessed by a well-concealed cover made of the stairs themselves.

Suggested Tools

Table saw

Backsaw

3/8" Drill

No. 8 screw bit

Phillips-head driver bit

Framing square

Nail puller

Hammer

Flat pry bar

Level

Tape measure

Hardware and Supplies

No. 8 X 1-3/4" wood screws

No. 10 X 1-1/2" wood screws

No. 10 X 2" wood screws

8-Penny finish nails

16-Penny sinker nails

5" Strap hinges

Construction adhesive

Cut List

1	Subfloor (plywood)	3/4" cut to size
7	Tongue & groove (or to match)	3/4" cut to size
2	Frame	1-1/2" X 1-1/2" X 30"
3	Frame	1-1/2" X 1-1/2" X 35-1/2"
2	Ledger	1-1/2" X 3-1/2" X 48"
2	Gas strut	1" X 12"
4	Angle brackets	1" X 1-1/2"
2	Corner braces	1-1/2" X 1-1/2" X 8"
2	Stringer (plywood)	1" X 16" X 21"
1	Backer (plywood)	3/4" X 8" X 48"
2	Backer (plywood)	3/4" X 16" X 22"
1	Grip	3/4" X 1" X 5"
1	Tread (plywood or to match)	3/4" cut to size
2	Risers (plywood)	3/4" cut to size

Construction Procedure

1. The dimensions in this project are mainly for reference, since your working space probably differs somewhat from the one shown here. The framing and procedures are typical of residential construction.

2. Establish that you can utilize the space beneath the landing by measuring the staircase and confirming what's below the head of the steps. A closet, or unused "dead space," offers a good opportunity; a hallway or a ceiling exposed to a room does not. Remove the flooring and subfloor from the landing, being watchful for wiring, plumbing, or heating ducts that might be running alongside the floor joists. Do not cut

through the framing or the stringers that support the stairs. If possible, use a pry bar rather than power tools at this stage to minimize damage in case you discover some unforeseen problem and have to put everything back.

3. If you can proceed, remove the top two treads and stair risers. Note here that you can make a perfectly usable trap door—and save considerable effort—by framing and hinging just the landing portion and leaving the steps intact. A flush-mounted pull ring would then be used as a lift handle rather than the grip shown.

4. Nail the ledgers to the floor joists on either side of the opening,

1-1/2" below the upper edge of each joist. This will allow room for the thickness of the door framing. If the door abuts a wall, first cut the 3/4" backers to size (so they'll come flush to the finished floor) and fasten them to the framing on that side before installing the ledger.

5. Cut the subfloor plywood to size and fasten the 30" side frame pieces to the lower edges of the panel starting 1-1/2" from the hinge end of the subfloor. Fasten with No. 10 X 2" wood screws. Attach the 35-1/2" frame pieces to the panel at each end.

6. Cut the stringer pieces to size using your existing steps as a model. Attach the stringers to the lower front edge of the subfloor panel, using No. 10 X 1-1/2" screws driven from the top. Strengthen the joints at the sides with 8" corner braces fastened with 1-1/2" screws. Fasten the remaining 35-1/2" frame member across the bottom of the subfloor at the point where the stringers end.

7. Cut the risers and treads to size to match the existing stairs. Fasten with 8-penny finish nails. Cut the 3/4" X 1" x 5" grip and attach it to the face of the front riser with No. 8 X 1- 3/4" wood screws.

8. Install the finish flooring in place on top of the subfloor. This can be glued with construction adhesive and blind-nailed with finish nails to hide the heads. Make sure it's cut to a length that allows at least 1/8" clearance from the flooring and backers at each end.

9. Place the assembled unit in position and adjust for equal clearance at the sides. Fasten the strap hinges to the wall and the flooring

about 24" apart with No. 10 wood screws.

10. Open the door and fasten the angle bracket to the door framing about 10" from the hinges with No. 8 X 1-1/2" screws. This distance can vary a bit according to your situation. Attach the gas struts, then establish where you need to fasten

the remaining set of support brackets to allow the door to close completely and open sufficiently. This is best accomplished if you get inside the space and mark the position with the door closed.

11. Finish the flooring material to match the existing floor.

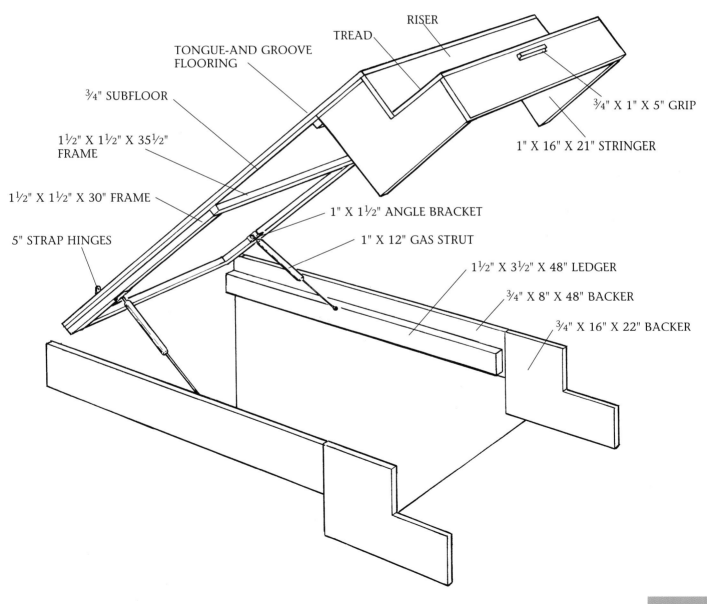

RISER

TREAD

TONGUE-AND GROOVE FLOORING

¾" SUBFLOOR

1½" X 1½" X 35½" FRAME

1½" X 1½" X 30" FRAME

5" STRAP HINGES

1" X 1½" ANGLE BRACKET

1" X 12" GAS STRUT

¾" X 1" X 5" GRIP

1" X 16" X 21" STRINGER

1½" X 3½" X 48" LEDGER

¾" X 8" X 48" BACKER

¾" X 16" X 22" BACKER

garden shed

Sometimes there's just not enough space in the house and things overflow to the outdoors. It wouldn't hurt to have this charming rustic garden shed ready to hold the stuff of substance: tools, firewood, bikes, barbecue grills, and bulky gardening equipment.

Suggested Tools

Table saw	1/2" Spade bit	Builder's line
Circular saw	3/4" Spade bit	C-clamps
Crosscut saw	Phillips-head driver bit	Hammer
Jigsaw	Tape measure	Chalk line
3/8" Drill	Framing square	Utility knife
No. 8 screw bit	Combination square	Adjustable wrench
1/4" Spade bit	Level	Posthole digger

Hardware and Supplies

15 lb. Builder's felt

Asphalt shingles or corrugated roofing

Roofing cement

No. 8 X 1-1/2" deck screws

1/2" X 14" Anchor bolts

6-Penny casing nails 6-penny sinker nails

8-Penny casing nails

16-Penny sinker nails

6-Penny siding nails

3/4" roofing nails

3/4" crushed stone

Concrete mix

6-mil Polyethylene sheeting

Utility tape

Extruded polystyrene insulation board

Exterior latex paint

Waterproof clear wood finish

Door hardware

Cut List

Commercial framing lumber is recommended for this project.

2	Treated posts	3-1/2" X 3-1/2" X 120"
2	Treated post	3-1/2" X 3-1/2" X 89"
2	Bottom plates	1-1/2" X 3-1/2" X 120"
2	Bottom plates	1-1/2" X 3-1/2" X 89"
17	Wall studs	1-1/2" X 3-1/2" X 77-1/2"
2	Top plates	1-1/2" X 3-1/2" X 132"
2	Top plates	1-1/2" X 3-1/2" X 92-1/2"
5	Collar ties	3/4" X 5-1/2" X 52-1/2"
2	Gable spacers	1-1/2" X 5-1/2" X 43"
5	Gussets	3/4" X 20" X 28-1/4"
5	Rafters	1-1/2" X 5-1/2" X 95"
5	Rafters	1-1/2" X 5-1/2" X 105"
1	Cripple stud	1-1/2" X 3-1/2" X 25-1/2"
1	Header	1-1/2" X 3-1/2" X 58-1/2"
1	Sill	1-1/2" X 3-1/2" X 58-1/2"
1	Cripple	1-1/2" X 3-1/2" X 15"
2	Trimmers	1-1/2" X 3-1/2" X 34"
2	Ledgers	1-1/2" X 1-1/2" X 11-1/2"
2	Soffit boards	11/16" X 6" X 89"
1	Soffit strip	1-1/4" X 1-1/4" X 89"
1	Window unit	28" X 34"
	Shiplap siding	11/16" X 6"
	Doors	48" X 77-1/2"
2	Stops	1/2" X 1-1/4" X 77"
1	Stop	1/2" X 1-1/4" X 48"
8	Corner boards	3/4" X 1-1/2" X 81"
2	Casing	3/4" X 1-1/2" X 77-1/2"
1	Casing	3/4" X 1-1/2" X 51"
2	Fascia	3/4" X 7-1/4" X 95"
2	Fascia	3/4" X 7-1/4" X 105"
2	Fretwork	3/4" X 11-1/4" X 95"
2	Fretwork	3/4" X 11-1/4" X 105"
2	Edge trim	3/4" X 1-1/2" X 95"
2	Edge trim	3/4" X 1-1/2" X 105"
7	Plywood sheathing	1/2" X 4' X 8'

Construction Procedure

1. Select a level site free of roots and rocks. Stake out an 8' X 10' rectangle and check for square by measuring and comparing corner-to-corner diagonal dimensions—they should be within 1/4" to 1/2". Measure in 12" from each end along each of the four sides and excavate an 8" hole with a posthole digger to a depth below the frost line in your locale, or a minimum of 16". Lay a 2" bed of crushed stone in each of the eight holes, then establish and mark the level for each of the eight piers. It may be necessary to nail together temporary box forms from 1-by lumber to raise the height of one or more piers in order to keep all eight at the same level. Use a line and a level stretched between points to check for level. Mix and pour concrete into the pier holes to level and insert one anchor bolt into each pier so the threads protrude 4" to 5". The bolts should be positioned 92-1/2" apart side to side and 116-1/2" apart end to end. Allow the concrete several days to cure.

2. Cut the 4 X 4 treated posts to the lengths indicated and drill 1/2" holes in each to correspond to the anchor bolts. Secure the beams to the pier bolts with nuts and washers.

3. Cut the studs and the top and bottom plates for each wall. These are best assembled on a level, flat surface such as a floor or driveway. Build one wall at a time, centering the back and side wall studs 30" apart, and the front wall door frame studs 49-1/2" apart (if you are using 48" doors as indicated). The end studs on the front wall are kept flush with the end of the plate. Fasten the face of the bottom plates to the lower ends of the studs with 16-penny sinkers; fasten the edge of the top plates to the upper ends of the studs in the same manner, using a toe-nailing technique. Measure the exact window header and sill length for the window wall and cut the trimmer and two cripple studs to fit the exact height of your window. Nail the trimmers, sill, and header in place to accommodate the window's rough opening, and nail the two cripple studs to the top and bottom plates. The window can be placed in any wall you wish.

4. Drill 3/4" relief holes into the bottom plates as needed to allow clearance for the protruding anchor bolts. With the help of a friend, tilt two adjoining walls up into position and temporarily nail the corner studs together. Adjust the bottom plates on the beams and use the level to check the walls for plumb. Nail the bottom plates down. Tilt the other two walls into place and plumb them. Nail the

plates down, then nail all corners, including top plates, together securely using 16-penny sinkers.

5. Prepare to cut one set of rafters, and a collar tie and gusset, as a pattern; note that the left side of the roof has a longer overhang than the right. First snap a chalk line on a smooth flat surface between points 48" apart. Then, from the midpoint of that line, measure up 39-1/2" and mark a point, using a framing square to make the second line perpendicular to the first. Lay one of the uncut rafters with its lower edge 1-1/2" below the right-hand mark and its upper corner just past the marked centerpoint. Use the blade of a square and a pencil to carry the centerline and the right-hand mark onto the face of the rafter. Measure 1-1/2" up from the edge along the lower line, then strike a perpendicular line toward the center to the edge of the rafter. Cut out the notch at that point with a handsaw, and cut along the line at the end to complete the rafter's ridge cut. Repeat this procedure with the longer left-hand rafter. Place both rafters over the marks on the floor, checking that the plumb or vertical cuts of the notches are 48" apart. Then cut the gusset piece to match the peak, and trim the ends of the collar tie. Cut the tails of both rafters to expose two 2-3/4" edges as shown. Screw the gusset and collar tie into place and fit the truss assem-

bly onto the side wall plates. Make adjustments as needed to fit.

6. Cut the remaining rafters, gussets, and collar ties using the pattern pieces. Assemble each truss set on the ground, then nail them to the top plates, one over each stud set. Keep them aligned temporarily by nailing to a 12' strip of 1-by. The front truss gets nailed to the cantilevered ends of the plates. Cut and nail in place the gable spacers on the faces of the front and back collar ties.

7. Cut and nail the 1/2" plywood roof sheathing to the trusses, bringing the edges flush with the outsides of the end rafters. (If you're using corrugated metal roofing, nail 1 X 4 strips 2' apart across the trusses.) Cut and nail the builder's felt over the plywood, then install the asphalt shingle courses using 3/4" roofing nails, beginning at the rafter tails and working toward the roof peak. Allow a 3/4" overhang at the sides. At the ridge, turn the shingles sideways and trim them as needed, then overlap each course by half before nailing. Secure the final piece with a liberal application of roofing cement.

8. Cut the fret boards to the length indicated, using the same ridge and tail angles as the rafters. Mark the 14"-repeating fretwork pattern as shown in the drawing onto each board, then cut the fretwork

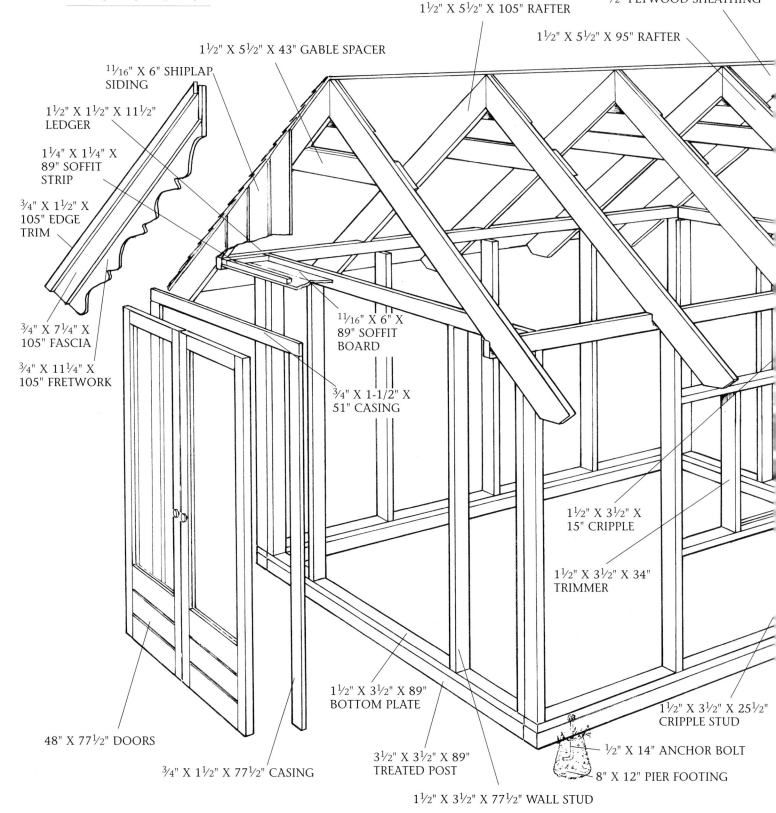

1½" X 5½" X 105" RAFTER

½" PLYWOOD SHEATHING

1½" X 5½" X 95" RAFTER

1½" X 5½" X 43" GABLE SPACER

11/16" X 6" SHIPLAP SIDING

1½" X 1½" X 11½" LEDGER

1¼" X 1¼" X 89" SOFFIT STRIP

¾" X 1½" X 105" EDGE TRIM

¾" X 7¼" X 105" FASCIA

¾" X 11¼" X 105" FRETWORK

11/16" X 6" X 89" SOFFIT BOARD

¾" X 1-1/2" X 51" CASING

1½" X 3½" X 15" CRIPPLE

1½" X 3½" X 34" TRIMMER

1½" X 3½" X 89" BOTTOM PLATE

1½" X 3½" X 25½" CRIPPLE STUD

48" X 77½" DOORS

¾" X 1½" X 77½" CASING

3½" X 3½" X 89" TREATED POST

½" X 14" ANCHOR BOLT

8" X 12" PIER FOOTING

1½" X 3½" X 77½" WALL STUD

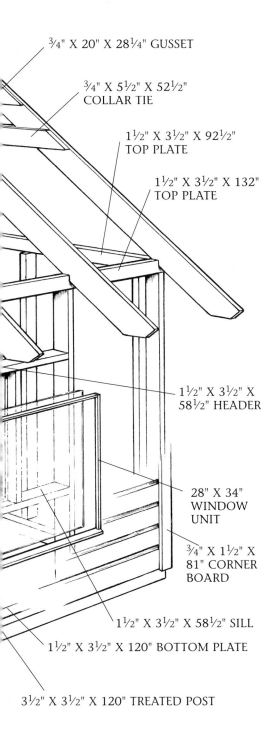

¾" X 20" X 28¼" GUSSET

¾" X 5½" X 52½" COLLAR TIE

1½" X 3½" X 92½" TOP PLATE

1½" X 3½" X 132" TOP PLATE

1½" X 3½" X 58½" HEADER

28" X 34" WINDOW UNIT

¾" X 1½" X 81" CORNER BOARD

1½" X 3½" X 58½" SILL

1½" X 3½" X 120" BOTTOM PLATE

3½" X 3½" X 120" TREATED POST

with a jigsaw. Paint the boards before fastening them—butted against the shingle overhang—to the end rafters with 6-penny casing nails. Cut the fascia boards and fasten them, using 6-penny nails, to the upper portion of the fret boards, so they extend 2" above the shingle line. Cut the edge trim, paint or seal it, and fasten it to the edges of the fascia, inside edge flush with the inside face of the boards.

9. Fit the window unit in place so the casing extends 3/4" past the framing; the siding will butt directly against this. Fasten it to the framing with 8-penny casing nails. Hang the doors directly to the framing using 3" butt hinges and cut and fit the stop material. Fasten it with 6-penny casing nails. Install the door hardware. Cut and fit the door casing so the jamb pieces butt against the lower edge of the header casing. Fasten with 6-penny nails.

10. Rip a 45-degree bevel into one edge of each corner board and nail them to the corner studs using 6-penny sinkers. Cut the two soffit ledgers and nail them to the upper inside faces of the cantilevered top plates using 6-penny sinkers. Cut the soffit boards and nail them to the ledgers using the siding nails.

11. Measure and cut each piece of horizontal siding to fit between the corner boards, or between the corner boards and window or door casing. Work from the bottom up to fasten the siding at the edges with 6-penny nails.

12. Measure and cut each piece of vertical siding to cover the gable ends of the roof. On the cantilevered end, fit a full-width 1" or 1-1/4" strip against the soffit and behind the vertical boards to keep the soffit from sagging. Fasten with 6-penny nails.

13. Trim and lay three 4' X 8' sheets of polystyrene insulation board onto the ground inside the shed so the edges butt together. Cover the board with a layer of 6-mil polyethylene and tape it at the joints and to the foundation beams. Cover the plastic sheeting to a depth of 2" or 3" with crushed stone, and level it with a rake.

14. Paint the shed's trim, doors, and siding in the color scheme you feel most comfortable with. As an option, you can use an outdoor stain to give the shed an even more rustic appearance.

Index

Metric Conversion Chart

One inch equals about two and a half centimeters. To convert inches to centimeters precisely, multiply the number of inches by 2.54. Otherwise, refer to the chart below for a very close and convenient estimation.

INCHES	CENTIMETERS
1/8	0.3
1/4	0.6
3/8	1.0
1/2	1.3
5/8	1.6
3/4	1.9
7/8	2.2
1	2.5
2	5.1
3	7.6
4	10.2
5	12.7
6	15.2
7	17.8
8	20.3
9	22.5
10	25.4
11	27.9
12	30.5
13	33.0
14	35.6
15	38.9
16	40.6
17	43.2
18	45.7
19	48.3
20	50.8
21	53.3
22	55.9
23	58.4
24	61.0
25	63.5
26	66.0
27	68.6
28	71.1
29	73.7
30	76.2
31	78.7
32	81.3
33	83.8
34	86.4
35	88.9
36	91.4